SCHEDULING
for Home Builders
with Microsoft® Project

SCHEDULING
for Home Builders
with Microsoft® Project

Third Edition

David A. Marchman

Tulio Sulbaran, Ph.D.

NAHB® National Association of Home Builders

Scheduling for Home Builders with Microsoft® Project, Third Edition

BuilderBooks, a Service of the National Association of Home Builders

Elizabeth M. Rich	Director, Book Publishing
Natalie C. Holmes	Book Editor
Nadica Matolic	Cover Design
BMWW	Composition
Sheridan Books Inc.	Printing
Gerald M. Howard	NAHB Chief Executive Officer
Mark Pursell	NAHB Senior Vice President, Exhibitions, Marketing & Sales
Lakisha Campbell, CAE	NAHB Vice President, Publishing & Affinity Programs

Disclaimer

This publication provides accurate information on the subject matter covered. The publisher is selling it with the understanding that the publisher is not providing legal, accounting, or other professional service. If you need legal advice or other expert assistance, obtain the services of a qualified professional experienced in the subject matter involved. Reference herein to any specific commercial products, process, or service by trade name, trademark, manufacturer, or otherwise does not necessarily constitute or imply its endorsement, recommendation, or favored status by the National Association of Home Builders. The views and opinions of the author expressed in this publication do not necessarily state or reflect those of the National Association of Home Builders, and they shall not be used to advertise or endorse a product.

Printed in the United States of America

16 15 14 13 12   1 2 3 4 5

Library of Congress Cataloging-in-Publication Data

Marchman, David A.
  Scheduling for home builders with Microsoft® project / David A. Marchman, Tulio Sulbaran.
    p. cm.
  Includes bibliographical references and index.
  ISBN-13: 978-0-86718-678-9 (alk. paper)
  ISBN-10: 0-86718-678-X (alk. paper)
  1. House construction—Data processing. 2. Production scheduling—Data processing.
3. Microsoft Project. I. Sulbaran, Tulio A. II. Title.
  TH4812.M2364 2012
  690'.8370685—dc23

                                                                              2011038710

For further information, please contact:

National Association of Home Builders
1201 15th Street, NW
Washington, DC 20005-2800
800-223-2665
www.BuilderBooks.com.

Contents

Figures

Introduction

Chapter 1

Chapter 2

Acknowledgments

David A. Marchman thanks the many home builders who have shared their philosophy about and experience with scheduling which informed this book. He also thanks Dr. Sulbaran for collaborating on this book. Finally, Mr. Marchman thanks his family for its continuing support: his wife, Janet S. Nelson; his son Dane and his family (Holly, Forrest, Sawyer, and Marilea Marchman); and his daughter Dee and her family (Josh, Kalah, Kalel, and Cohane Turnage).

Dr. Tulio A. Sulbaran thanks the many construction companies and construction organizations that provided priceless information for this book as well as opportunities for personal and professional growth. He thanks all his students, coworkers, and especially David A. Marchman, for collaborating on this book, and his mother Alida Gonzalez, wife Virginia, son Tulio Nicolas, and daughter Virginia Valentina "Tina" for their nurturing, support, understanding, and fun times together.

About the Authors

David A. Marchman, a consultant in scheduling, estimating, cost control, computer applications, safety, and legal issues, is a retired professor of construction engineering technology from the University of Southern Mississippi. He holds BS and MS degrees in building construction from the University of Florida and has worked in residential, commercial, and industrial construction. He taught courses in scheduling, quantity surveying, estimating, cost control, construction organization, and project management. He has also taught scheduling seminars for construction associations, builders, and contractors.

Tulio A. Sulbaran teaches estimating, scheduling, project management, and other construction courses in the School of Construction at the University of Southern Mississippi. He holds a doctorate from the Georgia Institute of Technology and has several years of international work experience in architecture, engineering, and construction. Dr. Sulbaran is a consultant for numerous companies including URS Corp, W.G. Yates Construction, Superior Asphalt, Mississippi Power, Jacobs, and others. He has been active in the Associated School of Construction, the American Council for Construction Education, the American Society for Engineering Education, the Associated Builders and Contractors, and other professional organizations. Dr. Sulbaran has taught many construction-related seminars and workshops at national and international conferences. In addition, he has published journal articles and several papers at national and international conferences.

Introduction

All home building projects require coordinating project plans and specifications, construction materials, craftspeople, construction equipment, and trade contractors to build the home. How you utilize these resources determines whether your project will run efficiently or end up in disarray. By developing a schedule at the beginning of the project, you can better plan and organize the tasks necessary to complete it. An organized schedule is a home builder's best tool for controlling project parameters and costs.

Microsoft® Project

Microsoft® Project allows you to define tasks and view the interrelationships between them to develop a home construction project schedule. You can also use the software to control and manage resources and costs. The software allows you to view the schedule according to various criteria, a particularly handy feature. For example, sorting the schedule by task responsibility will show the trade contractor or other individual(s) responsible for completing a task.

Microsoft® Project is flexible and easy to use. Even if trade contractors you work with don't have the latest technology for sharing information, the software allows you to print hard copies of schedules to share. Sharing is important. You must be able to disseminate information and receive feedback about the schedule for it to be effective. If you can't clearly communicate your schedule to other people it affects, the schedule is useless.

Microsoft® Project Ribbon

The new version of Microsoft® Project replaced traditional menus and tool-bars with a ribbon. This ribbon layout was designed to allow users to access common functions with fewer clicks. You can collapse and expand the ribbon to accommodate different screen resolutions. We recommend using the highest possible resolution when working in the practice files provided online (http://www.nahb.org/scheduling3e) to see the screen as described in the text. Figures I.1 and I.2 show the same Microsoft® Project file using screen resolutions, respectively, of 1600 × 1200, pictured in this book, and 1024 × 768. Notice that in figure I.2 (lower screen resolution) some screen option labels are truncated.

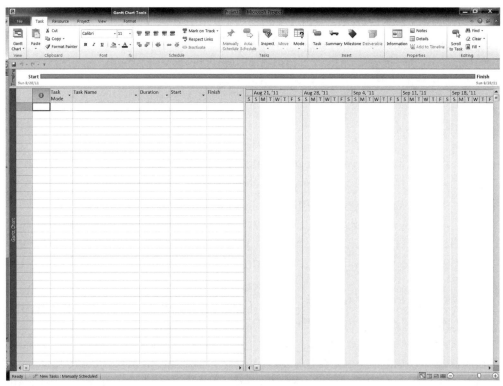

Figure I.1   View at 1600 × 1200

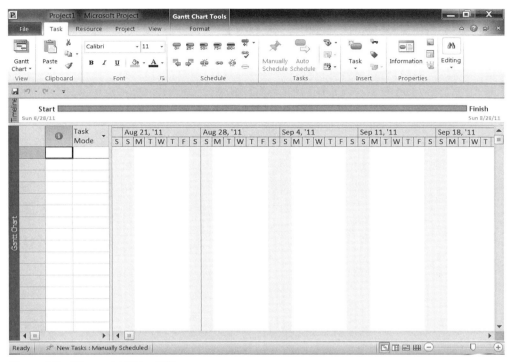

Figure I.2   View at 1024 × 768

Using the Practice Files

The sample schedules at http://www.nahb. org/scheduling3e allow you to practice the skills taught in each chapter. You must have Microsoft® Project 2010 installed on your computer to access the practice files. There

Get practice schedules online at http://www. nahb.org/scheduling3e

are two versions of Microsoft® Project—standard and professional. The standard version costs less because it is designed for a single user, whereas the professional version is designed to be loaded on a network server so multiple users can access it. The practice exercises in this book were created using Microsoft® Project Professional 2010. You can download a 60-day trial version of the standard software online at http://technet.microsoft.com/en-us/evalcenter/ee404758.aspx.

Microsoft® Project is a registered trademark of Microsoft® Corporation. Screen images shown in this book are reprinted with permission of Microsoft®.

Introduction to Scheduling

Project planning is a multistep process that begins well before you actually sit down at the computer to draft a schedule. With technology, construction codes, and financing evolving, home building projects are ever more complex and costly. You must continuously manage your time and resources, including specialized labor, materials, and construction equipment, through project completion. Planning and pacing construction allow you to use resources efficiently, meet contractual deadlines, and ensure a quality product. This chapter will help you understand the fundamentals of an effective home building schedule. You will learn about the following Microsoft® Project elements:

- Tasks
- Phases
- Milestones
- Gantt charts and reports
- Rough logic diagram
- Schedule

Benefits of Scheduling

The greatest marketing and sales collateral you have is your company's ability to complete a high-quality home on time and within budget. Moreover, the sooner you can complete a home, the faster you can move on to the next project. Delays are costly. They consume time, increase the amount of interest you'll pay on construction loans, and constrain your ability to get, or move on to, the next potentially profitable project.

Proper scheduling will prevent your wasting time and money on a project. By saving time, you can increase volume and profitability. An efficient construction company can produce more projects per year with the same management staff, which lowers overhead. Time is money!

Estimates and Schedules

There are four steps to successful residential project management:

1. **Planning.** In this phase, you decide how to execute a residential construction project. You create a rough diagram that identifies and defines activities and their relationship to other activities.
2. **Scheduling.** This phase includes estimating the time and other resources needed to execute the plan.
3. **Monitoring.** After construction starts, you monitor actual progress compared with the schedule and adjust resources as needed to complete the project.
4. **Controlling.** Finally, you document changes to the plan and schedule and inform others about schedule revisions. Changes to the scope of work, material delivery delays, and lower- or higher-than-expected productivity rates can impact the schedule.

Consistently following each step will ensure your projects remain under control. Two primary control documents will help you: the *estimate* and the *schedule*. The estimate defines a project's scope. It identifies materials quantities, labor hours, and equipment usage. Because you can measure these resources in dollars, the estimate also serves as the cost summary, or budget, for the project.

The schedule controls how you spend your time. Since time is money, both the resources and the time frame during which they are expended impact your profit margin. The estimate and the schedule interrelate and a change to one affects the other. Whereas the estimate computes, for example, hours of labor needed to complete a specific job, the schedule identifies when you will need workers. Successful home builders study both of these documents to conceptualize a project before they begin construction. This is the essence of planning.

Estimating, and to an even greater extent, scheduling, allow you to anticipate surprises and solve problems as you plan and before you expend resources, rather than making ad hoc decisions on the jobsite. Planning will smooth the construction process, minimize surprises, and prevent haphazardly spending resources.

Communication

Most home building projects require services from various experts and include myriad contractual relationships. Effective and ongoing communication will help you manage contracts and relationships well. When all project participants know the plan, understand their responsibilities, and are aware of your requirements and expectations, your project planning will pay off with a positive outcome. A schedule is useless if you are the only one who understands it. Keeping everyone informed is critical to maximizing the benefits of scheduling.

Tasks

The first step in developing a project schedule project is to identify tasks. A *task* is an activity that must be accomplished to meet a project goal. It requires time and, typically, other resources such as labor, materials, and equipment.

Many discrete and interrelated tasks come together in a residential construction project. Tasks (other than *milestones*) have five specific characteristics:

1. **They consume time.** How many days of work will the task require?
2. **They use resources.** How many cubic yards of concrete are in the footing?
3. **They have a start and finish.** The footing concrete pour cannot begin until workers install the footing rebar, and footing concrete must be finished before slab backfill can begin.
4. **You can assign them.** Each crew or trade contractor is responsible for completing a specific task or tasks.
5. **You can measure them.** You can determine at given intervals or specific points what percentage of a task is complete.

The project estimate, available historical information, and the project team's experience all contribute to defining tasks.

Task Names

The *task name* describes the activity. Task names must be concise and everyone who uses the schedule must understand them. This includes your workforce, trade contractors, the owner, and the designer.

Task Relationships

Task relationships encompass the activities that must occur before, after, or simultaneously with the defined task. Identifying these relationships provides logic to the schedule so it works. Task relationships also include the interaction of people or companies performing the work.

Phases

A *phase* is a group of related tasks. For example, the related tasks that comprise placing a brick wall are as follows:

- Purchase sand, masonry cement, and brick
- Rent mortar mixer and scaffolding
- Place brick
- Clean brick

By dividing the schedule into phases you can focus on one project element at a time, determine whether any tasks are missing from the phase, and report the schedule status with the correct level of detail.

Milestones

Milestones are tasks that do not represent actions. You can use milestones as interim goals to track the progress of a project. Having a house dried in is a milestone. You may have to reach a milestone to receive a progress payment.

Gantt Charts and Reports

The *Gantt chart* is an easy-to-read view of the schedule (fig. 1.1). The horizontal axis represents the *timescale*, and the vertical axis lists the tasks. The graph shows each task's duration on the timescale and when the task is to

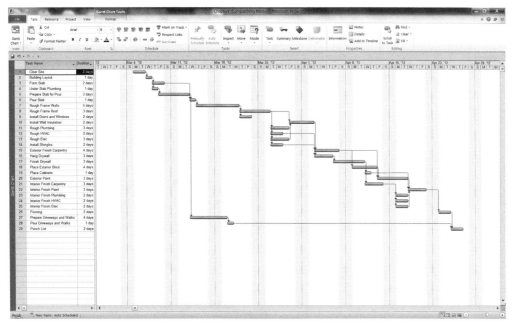

Figure 1.1   Gantt chart

start and end. You can name tasks broadly or narrowly to adequately describe the project.

Rough Logic Diagram

The rough logic diagram defines tasks and shows how they interrelate. Before you begin any development or construction, you must build your project on paper using a rough logic diagram.

After you develop and refine the rough logic diagram, use it to prepare a draft schedule. After all project participants review and accept it, it becomes your project plan.

Follow these three steps to prepare the diagram:

1. **Convene a meeting.** Include the superintendent, major foremen or forewomen, estimator, and major trade contractors. The group should use the estimate to build the project on paper. The group will identify tasks, estimate their durations, and note the relationships among tasks. Designate one attendee to record the meeting minutes. The meeting should take no more than two hours.
2. **Gather information.** You need to find out

- the home owner's time constraints;
- scopes of work for each trade (How many blocks does the masonry trade contractor have to place?);
- construction methods and procedures (Will the slab concrete shoot from the concrete truck, be pumped, or be dumped from a crane bucket?);
- productivity rates (How many blocks can the masonry crew place in an hour?);
- crew composition (the masonry crew comprises a foreman, three journeymen masons, and four laborers, for example);
- construction equipment (the masonry crew requires a mortar mixer);
- whether and when construction equipment will be available;
- whether and when materials will be available;
- when trade contractors are available;
- when fabricators are available;
- temporary facilities requirements; and
- permits and test requirements.

3. **Draw the diagram.** Use the information you gather to draw the rough logic diagram and show how tasks interrelate.

Schedule

You can use the diagram to draft a proposed project schedule. This schedule should include details about task durations, resource requirements, and costs. Follow these three steps to establish a schedule:

1. **Review the schedule.** The entire project team must accept the rough logic diagram. The team must agree with your concept, methods, and procedures for the construction project to run smoothly.
2. **Get buy-in.** As the home builder, you are responsible not only for coordinating and scheduling the work but also for resolving disputes. By meeting with trade contractors and suppliers in advance, you can modify the plan and reconcile differences. Be sure to obtain information from all parties whose work can impact the schedule.

3. **Accept the schedule.** Once you review the rough schedule with trade contractors and suppliers and they sign-off on it, it becomes the official project schedule.

Measuring Success

Each home building project has a start date, an end date, a unique set of characteristics, and specific tasks required to complete it. Ask the following questions to determine whether a project was successful:

- Did the project come in on budget?
- Did the project come in on time?
- Were your clients and employees satisfied?
- Did the project use company resources efficiently?

2

Creating the Microsoft® Project Schedule

This chapter will discuss basic Microsoft® Project attributes and capabilities. You will create a new project file, enter and organize activities, and manipulate the schedule view.

After you read this chapter and practice the skills, you will be able to

- create and open project files;
- save files;
- identify the Gantt chart;
- modify views;
- adjust timescales;
- add a task and enter its name;
- enter task length;
- enter milestones;
- link (connect related) tasks;
- enter task constraints; and
- identify the critical path.

Use the Chapter2.mpp file to practice these skills.

Creating and Opening Microsoft® Project Files

When you launch Microsoft® Project, a blank project file displays in the Gantt chart view (fig. 2.1). To create a new project, select File from the *ribbon* at the top of the screen (fig. 2.2). Then select New to create a project.

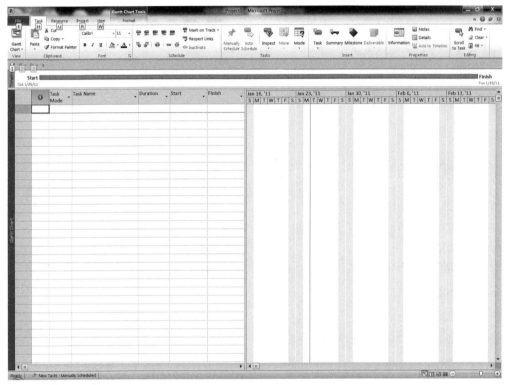

Figure 2.1   A blank project file in Gantt chart view

Figure 2.2   File view

Figure 2.3 Templates for creating new schedules

The screen shows Available Templates, files preconfigured to create new schedules (fig. 2.3). Click Blank project and the Create button (lower right portion of screen) and a blank schedule will appear.

Skill Practice 2.1 Entering the Project Date

1. To enter the project start date, click the Project tab and select the Project Information button. The Project Information dialog box opens (fig. 2.4).
2. Click the downward arrow in the Start date box to open a calendar, or manually type in the start date using the format shown in the software (day of the week and m/d/yy).
3. Use 3/5/12 as the project start date.
4. Click OK. An empty project file appears (fig. 2.5) with dates displayed at the top. This is the Gantt chart default view.
5. Select File on the ribbon.
6. Click Save. When you attempt to save the first time, the Save As dialog box will appear (fig. 2.6).

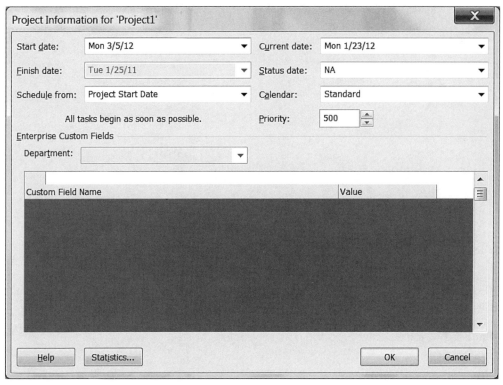

Figure 2.4   Project information dialog box

7. Type "Chapter 2 Exercise" in the File name field.
8. Click Save.

You will not save the changes you make to the practice files. However, when you are building schedules for your projects, you should always save your changes.

Gantt Chart

The Gantt chart is widely used to visualize home building projects (fig. 2.7). Each task or activity appears as a single horizontal bar. These bars display on a timescale that appears at the top of the chart. The length of an individual task bar represents the task's duration. This snapshot allows you to quickly assess the status of home building tasks. For example, figure 2.8 shows the Building Layout task cannot begin until its predecessor task, Clear Site, is complete. *Link lines* show the relationships among tasks. They allow you to see which task(s) must be completed before other task(s) can start.

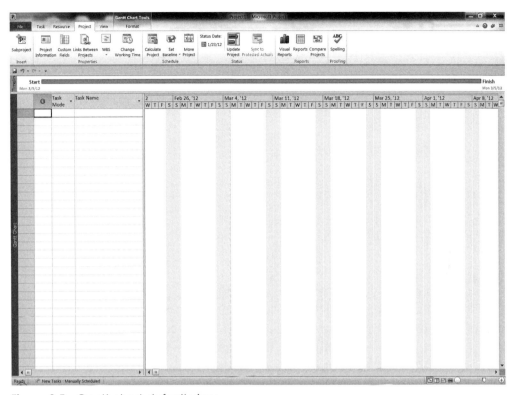

Figure 2.5 Gantt chart default view

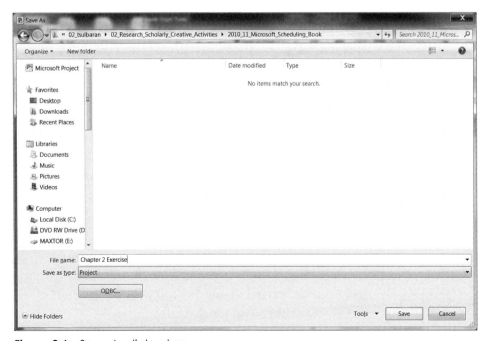

Figure 2.6 Save As dialog box

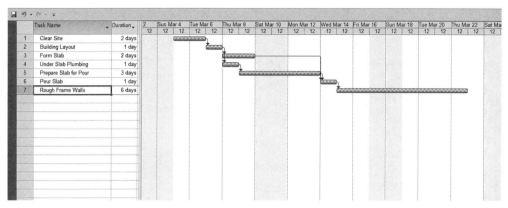

Figure 2.7 Gantt chart

Views

A *view* is the format in which you can enter and display information in Microsoft® Project. A single view is simply a single sheet, chart, graph, or form. A combination view simultaneously displays two views. For example, the Gantt chart view displays the entry table sheet view and the bar chart. You enter task information in the table on the left, and the bar chart on the right displays graphically, on a timescale, the information you entered.

Microsoft® Project offers three types of views:

- **Sheet view** displays task or resource information in rows and columns. Sheet view is useful for entering or viewing a large volume of information.

- **Chart/graph view** graphically represents your tasks or resources. Chart/graph view is useful when you need to present information visually without a lot of detail.

- **Form view** displays individual task or resource information. It helps you focus on detailed information about a specific task or resource.

To display any view, use the View tab on the ribbon (fig. 2.8). The View tab displays an icon for each of the eight most commonly used views.

Clicking the Other Views icon will present even more views to choose from. The seven most commonly used views are the following:

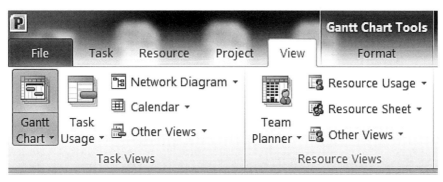

Figure 2.8 View tab

1. **Gantt chart** provides a list of tasks and related information, and displays a chart showing tasks and their durations on the timescale. Use this view to enter and schedule a list of tasks.

2. **Task usage** displays a list of tasks with their assigned resources grouped under each one. Use this view to see which resources are assigned to specific tasks and to keep track of resource usage.

3. **Network diagram** shows all tasks and task dependencies. This view allows you to create and fine-tune your schedule in a flowchart.

4. **Calendar** shows the project tasks and their duration by month. Use this view to show the tasks scheduled in a specific week or range of weeks.

5. **Tracking Gantt** provides a list of tasks with related information and a chart showing *baseline* and scheduled Gantt bars for each task. If you update a schedule, you can use this view to compare the *baseline schedule* with the actual schedule.

6. **Resource sheet** provides a list of resources and related information. Use this view to enter and edit resource information in a spreadsheet.

7. **Resource usage** provides a list of resources that show task assignments grouped under each resource. Use this view to show cost or work allocation information over time for each resource per assignment and combined resource usage.

To access more view options, select Other Views from the drop-down menu on the View tab of the ribbon and select More Views. The More Views dialog box appears displaying other view options.

Adjusting the Timescale

In addition to moving within a view to display additional project information, you can adjust the Timescale unit and display additional graphical information as follows:

- Select the Timescale drop-down menu (fig. 2.9).
- Select Timescale from the Timescale drop-down menu to access the Timescale dialog box (fig. 2.10).

The timescale extends across the top of the Gantt chart. It shows when a task takes place. The timescale includes a top tier, a middle tier, and a bottom tier. The top tier displays large units of time, the middle tier displays smaller units of time, and the bottom tier displays the smallest units of time.

Skill Practice 2.2 Adjusting the Timescale

1. Open the Chapter2.mpp file.
2. Use the Zoom In and Zoom Out buttons on the toolbar to adjust the timescale tiers. The Zoom In button decreases the timescale into smaller units (down to hours in 15-minute increments) to give you a more detailed view. The Zoom Out button increases the timescale to larger units (up to years in 6-month increments) to give you a broader view.
3. Now adjust the timescale using the Timescale dialog box: double click on the calendar bar of the Gantt chart, and change the Size % option.
4. Close the file without saving your changes.

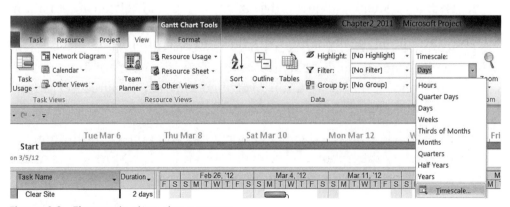

Figure 2.9 Timescale drop-down menu

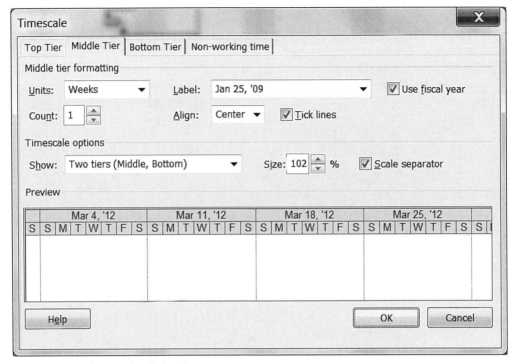

Figure 2.10   Timescale dialog box

Entering Task Names

To input a list of tasks, you must enter each one in the Task Name column of the Entry table (fig. 2.11). You can do this in Gantt chart view or in other views with a Task Name column. Each task in the task list is associated with a Task Identification (ID) number. As you enter tasks, Microsoft® Project automatically assigns the task ID numbers and enters them in the gray row headings on the left side of the Gantt chart view. When you edit the task list the software automatically renumbers tasks to keep the items in order. To delete a task, select it, click the right mouse button and select Delete Task.

Skill Practice 2.3 Entering Tasks

1. Use the Chapter 2 Exercise file you created to enter the following tasks:
   - Clear Site
   - Building Layout

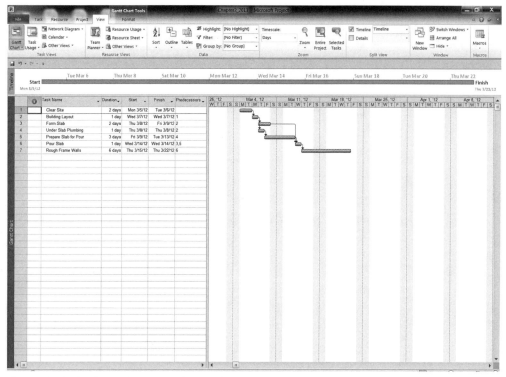

Figure 2.11   Task ID, Name, and Duration columns

- Form Slab
- Under Slab Plumbing
- Prepare Slab for Pour
- Pour Slab

2. Delete the Prepare Slab for Pour task.
3. Save the file.

Entering Task Duration

You must enter a duration estimate, or the amount of time you project each task will take. You can specify these durations in minutes, hours, days, or weeks as working time or elapsed time. A unit of working time is confined to the hours available in the day and the number of days that resources are actually being used. A unit of elapsed time includes both working and nonworking time based on a 24/7 schedule. One day is the default duration. As you enter tasks, Microsoft® Project automatically enters the default duration estimate in the Duration column. You can change the default duration by entering a new value and unit of time in the Duration field for the task.

Skill Practice 2.4 Adding Task Durations

1. Using the Chapter 2 Exercise file you saved, enter the following task durations:
   - Clear Site: 2 days
   - Building Layout: 1 day
   - Form Slab: 2 days
   - Under-Slab Plumbing: 1 day
   - Prepare Slab for Pour: 3 days
   - Pour Slab: 1 day
2. Save the file.

You can enter task information by selecting a field in the Entry table or by selecting the Task ID heading. By default, the cursor moves one row down when you press the Enter key while working in a field. When you press Tab, the cursor moves one field to the right. When you press Shift+Tab, the cursor moves one field to the left. The cursor will continue to cycle through the selected row until you select another field. You can also use the mouse or the keyboard arrows to move from field to field in the Entry table.

As you develop your schedule and the home building project progresses, you may need to add new tasks.

Skill Practice 2.5 Adding More Tasks

1. Using the Chapter 2 Exercise file, select the Pour Slab task row.
2. Right click the mouse and select Insert Task.
3. Type the new task name Prepare Slab for Pour.
4. Enter a duration of 3 days.
5. Save your changes.

Moving a Task

Follow these steps to move a task:

1. Move the mouse pointer over the Task ID (the number to the left of the task) and press the left mouse button, (the activity will be highlighted and the pointer will change to a four-pointed arrow).
2. Hold the left mouse button down, move the task to the new location and release the mouse button. Microsoft® Project will automatically insert a row at the new location, put the new task in the new location and delete the task from the prior location.

Entering Recurring Tasks

A task that occurs repeatedly is a *recurring task*. A recurring task could be a weekly meeting, a status report, or a regular inspection. Creating a recurring task saves time you would spend manually typing the task and duration. Use the Recurring Task Information dialog box to specify parameters for the recurrence. On the Task tab, select the Task drop-down menu (fig. 2.12) to obtain the Recurring Task Information dialog box (fig. 2.13).

Skill Practice 2.6 Creating a Recurring Task

1. Open Chapter2.mpp.
2. Select the Clear Site task row.
3. Select Task on the ribbon, and then select Recurring Tasks from the drop-down menu. A dialog box appears.

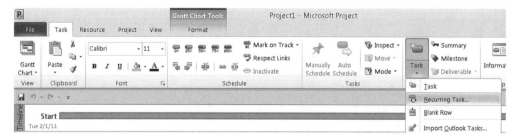

Figure 2.12 Task drop-down menu

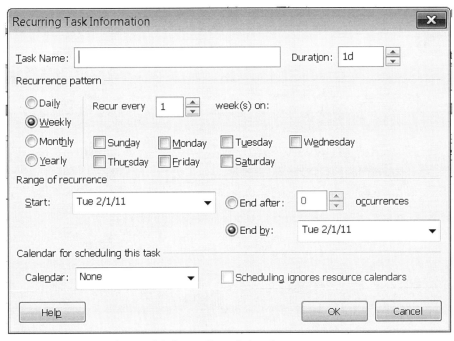

Figure 2.13 Recurring Task Information dialog box

4. Type "Staff Meeting" in the Task Name field.
5. Set the task to occur weekly.
6. Specify the recurrence pattern to occur on Monday.
7. Click OK.
8. Close the file without saving your changes.

Entering Milestones

As discussed in Chapter 1, milestones represent the completion of an event, phase, or other measurable goal in a home-building project. You can add milestones to mark the start or finish of significant portions of your home building project. Milestones have a duration of zero. Select the task where the milestone is needed (fig. 2.14). When a task becomes a milestone, the bar for that task changes to a diamond-shaped marker with the date the milestone occurs to the left of the marker (fig. 2.15).

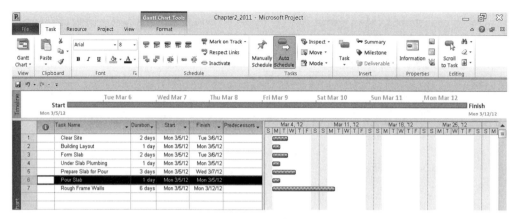

Figure 2.14   Pour Slab task selected to place milestone before it

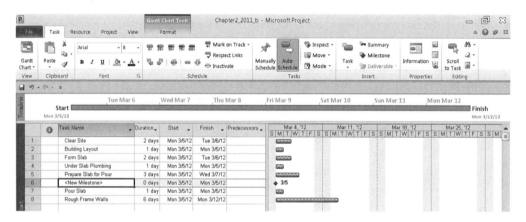

Figure 2.15   New milestone inserted

Skill Practice 2.7 Adding Milestone Activities

1. In the Chapter 2 Exercise file, select the Pour Slab task.
2. Select Task on the ribbon.
3. Select Recurring Tasks. The Recurring Task Information dialog box appears.
4. Name the new milestone activity "Inspect Slab" (fig. 2.16).
5. Enter zero (0) in the Duration field.
6. Notice the diamond-shaped milestone marker on the Gantt chart.

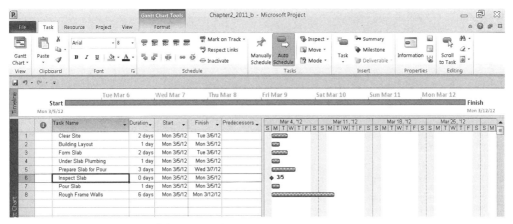

Figure 2.16 Milestone activity named

Entering Task Links

When you enter a task, Microsoft® Project automatically schedules it to begin on the project start date. You can link tasks according to their dependencies as follows:

- Click the first activity to be linked.
- Hold the Ctrl key while selecting other tasks to be linked.
- When you finish your selections, click the Link button on the ribbon (fig. 2.17).

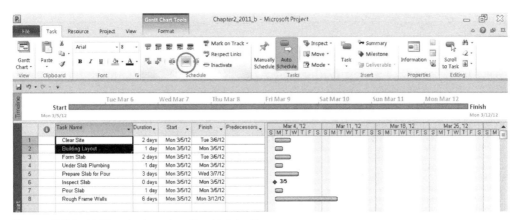

Figure 2.17 Linking tasks using the Link button

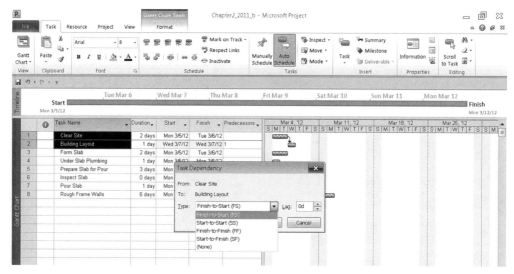

Figure 2.18 Task dependency dialog box

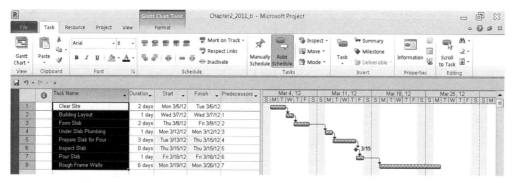

Figure 2.19 Linked tasks displayed on Gantt chart

Microsoft® Project will automatically reschedule the start dates as needed. The software also sets the completion dates for each task (fig. 2.18), moves the task bars in the Gantt chart view to the appropriate date(s) on the time-scale, and draws link lines to display the dependency (fig. 2.19).

There are four types of task dependencies: *finish-to-start, finish-to-finish, start-to-start,* and *start-to-finish.*

- **Finish-to-start.** The next task starts as the previous task is completed. This is the most common task dependency.

- **Finish-to-finish.** Both tasks may finish at the same time.

- **Start-to-start.** Both tasks may start at the same time.
- **Start-to-finish.** The start of one task depends on completing another task. This is the least common task dependency.

A task that must start or finish before another task can begin is called a *predecessor* task. A task that depends on the start or finish of a preceding task is called a *successor* task. Each dependency can either lengthen or shorten the schedule's duration. For example, a finish-to-start dependency extends the duration because one task must finish before the other can start. The start-to-start and finish-to-finish dependencies can shorten the duration because they overlap.

Linking Tasks to Create Task Dependencies

Linking tasks creates a default *finish-to-start dependency*. You can display the Task Dependency dialog box by double clicking a link line between tasks. Once you have entered all tasks in the default dependency type, you can identify and address the tasks that are an exception to the common finish-to-start dependency. You can unlink unrelated tasks and phases and link tasks not listed consecutively in the task list. You can also link tasks to a single predecessor and successor or to multiple predecessors and successors. Link a few tasks and observe how these links affect the schedule. Then link all tasks in a finish-to-start dependency. Next, unlink noncontiguous tasks. Note how the tasks within a group automatically move back in time when you remove a link between tasks.

Skill Practice 2.8 Linking Tasks

1. Open the Chapter2.mpp file.
2. To link tasks, select them and click the Auto Schedule button in the Format tab on the ribbon.
3. Click Link Tasks on the Task tab of the ribbon to show the relationships.
4. Link the following tasks: Clear Site, Building Layout, Form Slab, and Under-Slab Plumbing.
5. To unlink tasks, select them and click the Unlink Tasks button on the ribbon.

6. Unlink the tasks you just linked.
7. To link noncontiguous tasks, select the first task to be linked and press CTRL, then select the next task to be linked, and click the Link Tasks button on the Task tab of the ribbon.
8. Link the tasks Clear Site and Under-Slab Plumbing (fig. 2.20).

You can also link tasks by dragging and dropping them on the Gantt chart:

1. Place the mouse pointer over the center of the Gantt chart bar representing the first task in the link. (The pointer changes to a four-headed arrow.)
2. Drag down to the center of the Gantt bar for the second task in the link. (As you drag over the task bars, the pointer changes to a chain link and a Screen Tip displays, indicating the link to be established.)
3. Release the mouse button when the Screen Tip displays correct information.
4. Close the file without saving your changes.

Changing Task Dependencies

To change the dependency type, use the Task Dependency dialog box or any view that displays the Type field. The dialog box confirms which tasks the link line connects and displays the current dependency. You can use the Type box to change the dependency. When you change a task dependency, Microsoft® Project redraws the link line on the Gantt chart to reflect the change. Link lines allow you to quickly identify task dependencies.

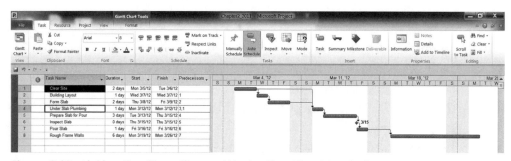

Figure 2.20 Linking the Clear Site and Under Slap Plumbing tasks

Figure 2.21   Task Details form

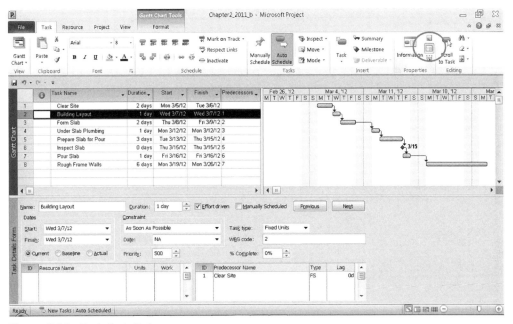

Figure 2.21   Task Details form

Task Details Form

You can also view information about task dependencies in the Task Details form on the Task tab under the Details button (fig. 2.21). The Task Details form provides information about an individual task, including its start and finish dates, predecessor task, and dependency type. You can view just the Task Details form or you can select the Task Entry view to see both the Task Form and the Gantt chart views. To see the Task Entry view, click the View tab; then click Task Usage/More Views/Task Entry/Apply.

Changing Task Dependencies

To change the dependency type, use the Type field on the Task Details Form below the Gantt chart (fig. 2.22). You can choose from the following options: Finish to Finish (FF), Finish to Start (FS), Start to Finish (SF), or Start to Start (SS). When you change a task dependency, Microsoft® Project redraws the relationship lines on the Gantt chart.

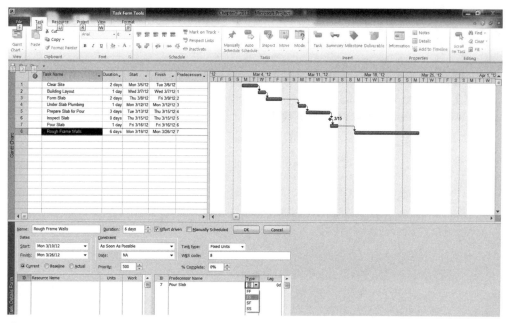

Figure 2.22   Choosing the task dependency type

Lead Time and Lag Time

In addition to changing the dependency type, you can refine the schedule further by entering lead time and lag time on the Details form or in the Task Dependency dialog box (fig. 2.23). To access the dialog box, double-click the *relationship line* between two selected activities on the Gantt chart. Lead time creates an overlap in a task dependency that can shorten a project's duration. For example, if you specify a lead time of one day on a finish-to-start dependency, the two tasks overlap by one day. In other words, the last day of the first task occurs while the first day of the second task takes place. Lag time creates a delay, or gap, in the task dependency that can lengthen the project duration. For example, if you specify a lag time of one day on a finish-to-start dependency, there is a one-day gap between the tasks. In other words, the first task finishes, a day goes by, and the second task starts. Lead time moves the start of the successor task back in time, and lag time moves the start of the successor task forward in time.

The Lag field specifies both lead and lag. Lead displays as a negative number because the project duration is shortened. In contrast, lag is displayed as a positive number because the project duration is lengthened. You enter lead time and lag time in the Lag box on the Task Dependency dialog box or in any view that displays the Lag field.

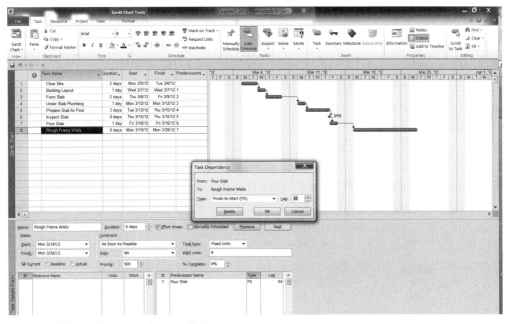

Figure 2.23   Task dependency dialog box

Skill Practice 2.9 Entering Task Lag Time

There are two ways to specify lag time:

1. Open Chapter2.mpp.
2. Double-click the link line between Pour Slab and Rough Frame Walls.
3. Press TAB to move to the Lag box.
4. Select 1d to reflect the amount of lag time.
5. Click OK.
6. Notice how the link line between the tasks moves forward on the timescale.

Or,

1. Double click the link line between the previous tasks.
2. Press TAB to move to the Lag box.
3. Type 2 to reflect the amount of lag time.
4. Click OK.
5. Notice how the link line between the tasks moves back on the timescale.
6. Close the file without saving your changes.

Entering Task Constraints

The default task start date that Microsoft® Project applies to each task corresponds with the start date of the home building project. Likewise, the default setting for all task completion dates is the project completion date. When you apply relationships to tasks and assign durations, the program sets start and finish dates according to their task dependencies. You can apply either *flexible* (not date specific) or *inflexible* (date specific) constraints on specific tasks.

The Microsoft® Project default for task constraints is As Soon As Possible. You must understand how and when to deviate from this default. For example, you may need to assign a constraint of As Late As Possible for less critical tasks that will need an often-used resource so the resource will be available when needed for critical-path tasks. Other constraints include: Start No Earlier Than, Finish No Earlier Than, Start No Later Than, and Finish No Later Than.

Skill Practice 2.10 Adding Constraints

1. Open the Chapter2.mpp file.
2. Press F5 to access the Go To data box (fig. 2.24).
3. Type 8 in the ID field.
4. Click OK.
5. Double click the Rough Frame Walls task. The Task Information dialog box appears.

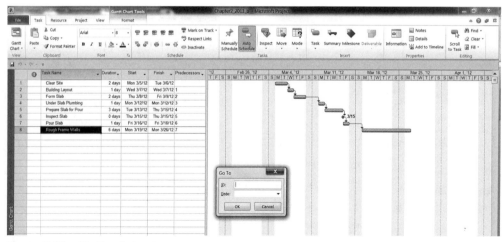

Figure 2.24 Go To dialog box

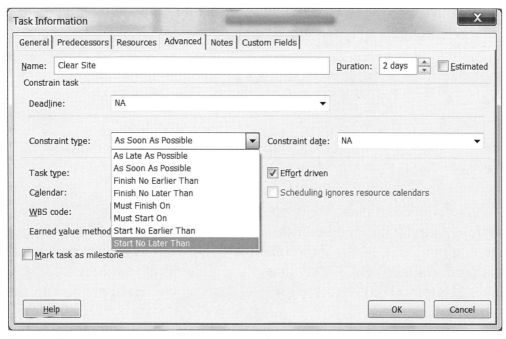

Figure 2.25 Task dependency; lag and lead time

6. Check the finish date in the General tab in the Task Information dialog box. The date should read "Mon 3/5/12."
7. Click the Advanced tab (fig. 2.25).
8. Click the drop-down arrow in the Constraint type field.
9. Select As Soon As Possible.
10. Click OK.
11. Close the file without saving your changes.

Identifying Critical Tasks

The *critical path* identifies *critical tasks* for finishing a project on schedule. Lengthening the duration of a critical task or delaying its start date will impact a project's completion date. Critical tasks form a critical path through the home building project. After you format a residential construction project schedule to display the critical path, you can reduce or lengthen the overall project's duration by changing the duration, dependencies, or resources used by critical tasks.

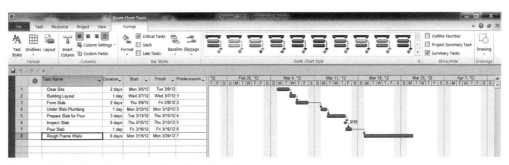

Figure 2.26   Gantt chart with critical path

Select the Gantt chart Tools tab on the ribbon to format the Gantt chart to automatically display the critical path. Click the Critical Tasks box to select it (fig. 2.26). When you format the Gantt chart to display the critical path, critical task bars display in red and noncritical task bars display in blue. The critical path automatically updates as you make changes to the project schedule.

Skill Practice 2.11 Displaying the Critical Path

1. Open Chapter2.mpp.
2. Click Gantt chart Tools on the ribbon.
3. Click Critical Tasks to select it.
4. Save your changes.

Entering Sort/Filter/Group Tasks

To meet the needs of specific users of your schedule, you may want to filter (only show tasks limited by some limiting criteria) or sort the tasks by some limiting criteria. For example, filtering permits you to provide the electrical trade contractor a schedule highlighting only electrical tasks or provide the rough carpentry crew with only the information necessary to complete its work.

Sort

You can sort tasks by start date, finish date, priority, cost, or ID number. To change sort criteria, select the View tab on the ribbon and the Sort button (fig. 2.27).

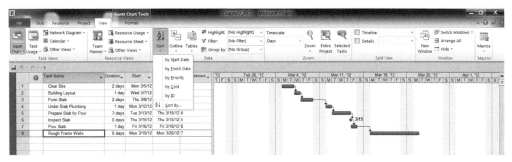

Figure 2.27   Sort options

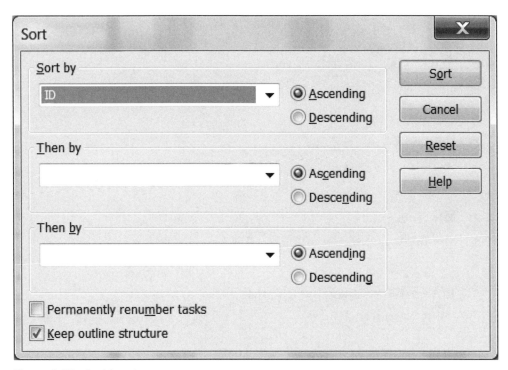

Figure 2.28   Sort levels

Select Sort by. A box appears with options for sorting tasks (fig. 2.28). You can choose up to three sort criteria and the order in which to apply them.

You can also filter tasks to view them selectively. To filter tasks, click the View tab on the ribbon. Click the downward arrow in the box next to Filter. A drop-down menu appears with the following options (fig. 2.29):

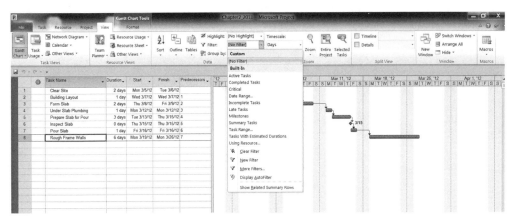

Figure 2.29   Filter: options

- Active Tasks (the default setting)
- Completed Tasks
- Critical
- Date Range
- Incomplete Tasks
- Late Tasks
- Milestones
- Summary Tasks
- Task Range
- Tasks With Estimated Durations
- Using Resource

You can access other filter options by selecting More Filters.

Group

Microsoft® Project can group tasks by criteria, which is helpful in consolidating tasks with common features. Click the View tab on the ribbon and the downward-facing arrow in the box next to Group by: (fig. 2.30). You will see the following options:

- No Group (default)
- Active v. Inactive

- Auto Scheduled v. manually Scheduled
- Complete and Incomplete Tasks
- Constraint Type
- Critical
- Duration
- Duration then Priority
- Milestones
- Priority
- Priority Keeping Outline Structure
- Resource
- Status

You can access other filter options by selecting More Groups.

Skill Practice 2.12 Sorting, Filtering, and Grouping Tasks

1. Open Chapter2.mpp.
2. Sort the schedule by Start Date.
3. Filter the schedule by Incomplete Tasks.
4. Group the schedule by Constraint Type.
5. Close the file without saving your changes.

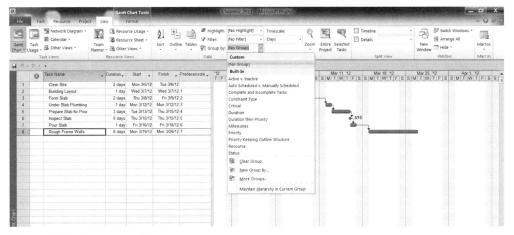

Figure 2.30   Group: options

Schedule Options

The Project Options dialog box is an important feature. It allows you to control your schedule's environment. You can set defaults for how the schedule will display, what calculations the program will use, how the schedule will be saved, and to otherwise customize functions. Select the File tab on the ribbon. Select Options (fig. 2.31). The Project Options dialog box appears (fig. 2.32). You can change the default view, how calculations are performed, spelling rules, and other features of your schedule using these options:

- General
- Display
- Schedule
- Proofing
- Save
- Language
- Advanced
- Customize Ribbon
- Quick Access Toolbar
- Add-Ins
- Trust Center

Figure 2.31   Project options

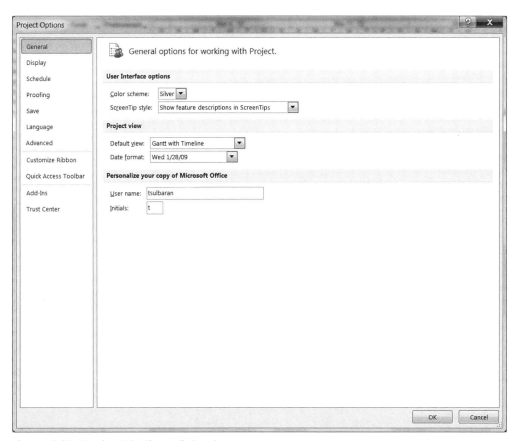

Figure 2.32   Project Options dialog box

Knowing the Basics

Now that you understand the basic features of Microsoft® Project, you can better manage your construction schedule. You can consolidate tasks to increase efficiency, filter information to simplify communication with trades, and use various views to begin to manage time, labor, and materials more effectively. Communication is among the most challenging tasks a home builder faces during a construction project. To communicate effectively, you must become proficient in sorting, filtering, and simplifying the schedule to provide information as needed to specific schedule users.

3

Managing Resources and Costs

This chapter will show you how to use Microsoft® Project to allocate resources like time, labor, and equipment efficiently to meet profit goals. You will learn how to establish the labor, material, and where applicable, the construction equipment requirements for each task so you can evaluate and refine the project schedule. After reading this chapter and performing the Skill Practices, you will be able to

- create a resource list;
- assign costs to the resource list;
- assign resources and costs to tasks; and
- add resources notes.

Use the Chapter3.mpp file to practice these skills.

Controlling Resources

You must control all of your project's resources. This means managing labor hours, bulk materials, construction equipment, and permanent equipment efficiently to save time and money. Your project's success depends on being able to get the maximum value from the time and money you spend. Managing details, monitoring costs and time, and controlling waste will help you be a successful builder.

Loading Resources

Microsoft® Project helps you control resources because the program allows you to enter the workers, materials, and construction equipment you plan to use to use before you begin building. When you input and assign the labor resources to tasks in advance, you can identify which tasks must be accomplished on a particular day and how many and what type of workers each job requires. Dividing the larger project into smaller tasks—each with its own beginning and ending—helps you monitor progress and evaluate performance.

Managing Resource Limits

A *resource limit* is the maximum amount of a resource available. Therefore, if a person serves a unique function on a project, the limit is one *unit*. If five workers from one craft or trade are available, then the limit is five units. Resource limitations impact task relationships and project scheduling. If a resource is overallocated, Microsoft® Project can reschedule the activities so the resources are not overcommitted. This is *leveling*. The project schedule changes to accommodate resource limits.

Controlling Spending

Because your most important resource is money, scheduling and controlling the expenditure of funds is critical to project success. You must determine how much money you will need for each task and when you will need it. Although the home owner ultimately pays for a project, you need money to pay for construction until you receive a draw on a construction loan or close on a finished home. When you have a sound estimate, accurate cash flow projections, and a well-planned payment system, you can finance a project's construction without borrowing funds. You can maintain a positive cash flow and avoid withdrawing money from interest-earning accounts.

Each project should stand on its own as a profit center. Controlling each of the following activities will help you maintain a positive cash flow:

- Payment request to owner
- Labor productivity and costs
- Material and supplies cost
- Trade contractors

- Overhead costs
- Payment of funds

Cash Flow

A home builder needs funds to build projects and to run business operations. Payroll, materials, supplies, and construction equipment require cash.

Therefore, controlling the expenditure of funds is as important as controlling time. Most home building project contracts call for the builder to be paid monthly or upon completion of predetermined phases of work. Ultimately, you must complete the project satisfactorily for the owner. You must also ensure funds are properly spent and you are paid according to project progress.

Two Types of Schedule

An important function of a schedule is to evaluate a project's physical progress. To do that, you must create a baseline schedule that will operate efficiently and then monitor physical progress to determine whether it aligns with the plan. There are two ways to determine physical progress. One uses a *task cost-loaded schedule*, which breaks down home construction cost estimates by task (50–200 tasks comprise the typical home construction schedule). The second uses a *schedule of values*, which divides the home into three or four major components (e.g., slab poured, home dried in, and home finished) with percentages (e.g., 30%) assigned to each. The task cost-loaded schedule allows the builder and home owner to communicate about a home's physical progress in detail. The task cost-loaded schedule shows the completion of tasks, and more detailed information on costs consumed than a schedule of values, so the home owner can more accurately judge the percentage of project completion that determines the payment to the home builder. Both the builder and the owner, then, benefit from having resources and costs assigned to project tasks in advance. Moreover, many home owners now require task cost-loaded schedules.

Creating Resource Lists

You may assign applicable resources to each task to control the expenditure of the task resources and ensure that the task is completed successfully. A given task may require one or many resources. Remember that resources include people, equipment, materials, and other necessities such as permits.

As with tasks, you can name resources generally or in detail. For example, a resource name can be an occupational title, such as "laborer," or it can include a specific proper name, such as "Mark Bounds, assistant superintendent." You decide how much detail to include. Your naming style should be consistent. For example, in the list of resources the home builder may want to use the generic descriptor "electrical trade" for all schedules or customize descriptors to a specific home, such as "Jones Electric."

Defining Resources

The first step in tracking labor, costs, and home completion is to create a resource list. You can easily add information about your resources in Microsoft® Project Resource Sheet view. Click on the View tab of the ribbon and select the Resource Sheet (fig. 3.1).

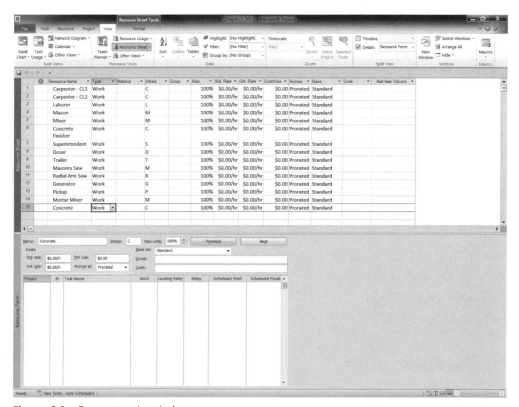

Figure 3.1   Resource sheet view

Skill Practice 3.1 Entering Resources

Open a blank Microsoft® Project file and follow these eight steps to enter a resource:

1. Select Resource Sheet from the View tab on the ribbon.
2. Type the resource names listed in figure 3.1 in the Resource Name column.
3. In the Type column, classify all resources as either Work (resources that do something, such as labor or construction equipment) or Material (resources that are consumed, such as brick). Use the pull-down menu in the Type field to select between the choices of Work, Material, or Cost. Microsoft® Project needs to know whether a resource is classified as work or material in order to calculate its usage correctly. Note that in figure 3.2, Laborer is classified as a Work type resource and Concrete is a Material resource. Classify the resources you just typed to match figure 3.2.

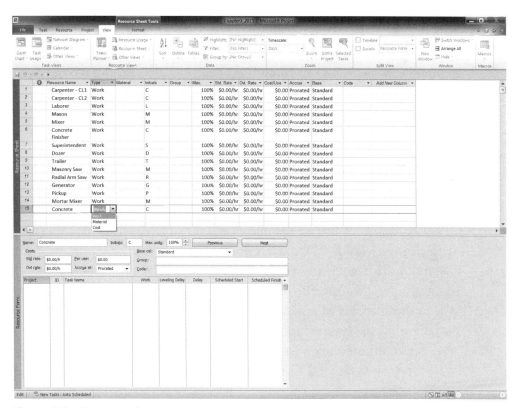

Figure 3.2 Resource type

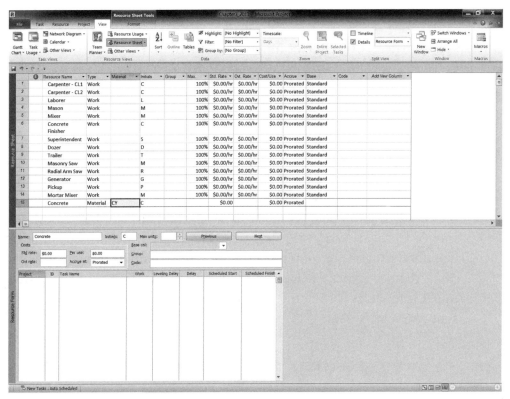

Figure 3.3 Material unit of measure

4. Microsoft® Project also needs to know how to measure resource usage. If the resource type is material, type the unit of measure in the Material column (fig. 3.3). If you select Work in the Type column, Microsoft® Project will not allow a unit of measure in the Material column. For the Concrete Material resource, type CY to indicate cubic yards as the unit of measure in the Material column. Common measurements for other materials are SF (square foot), LF (linear foot), or ton.
5. In the Initials column, type an abbreviation for the resource (C for Concrete). This will help you filter and edit the resources later.
6. To designate a resource group, type the group name in the Group field for each resource. For example, the Masonry Crew includes a mason, a mixer, a masonry saw, and a mortar mixer (fig. 3.4).
7. The Max. column shows the percentage of time a Work type resource will spend on a task. If one person works full time on a task, enter 100% in the column on the line that corresponds to the Work type resource. If you assigned a person to spend half of his or her time

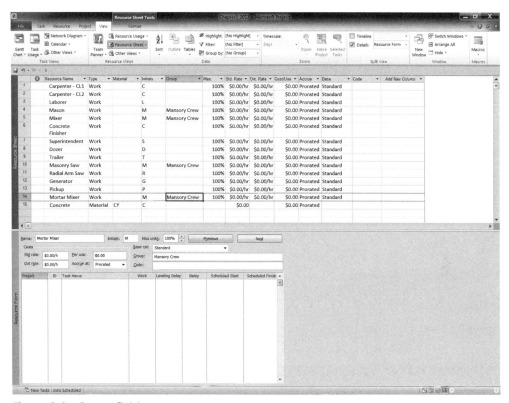

Figure 3.4 Group field

working on a task, then you would type 50% in the Max. field. Entering 400% in the Max. column for the Carpenter CL1 Work resource type allocates up to four carpenters. This means four carpenters is the maximum number that could be assigned to any task (fig. 3.5). Just as you cannot enter a unit of measurement for a Work resource, you cannot enter anything in the Max. column for a Material resource. Complete the Max. column as shown in figure 3.5.

8. The Std. Rate column applies to both Work and Material resources. For a Work resource, type the cost per period of time in the Std. Rate field. For example, the standard rate for the Laborer is $8 per hour and the overtime rate is $12 per hour (fig. 3.6). For a Material resource, input the unit cost in the Std. Rate field. The Concrete resource has quantity units of CY (cubic yards) and a Std. Rate of $50 (fig. 3.7). This means that the resource costs $50 per cubic yard. For Work resources, you can also add an overtime rate in the Ovt. Rate column.

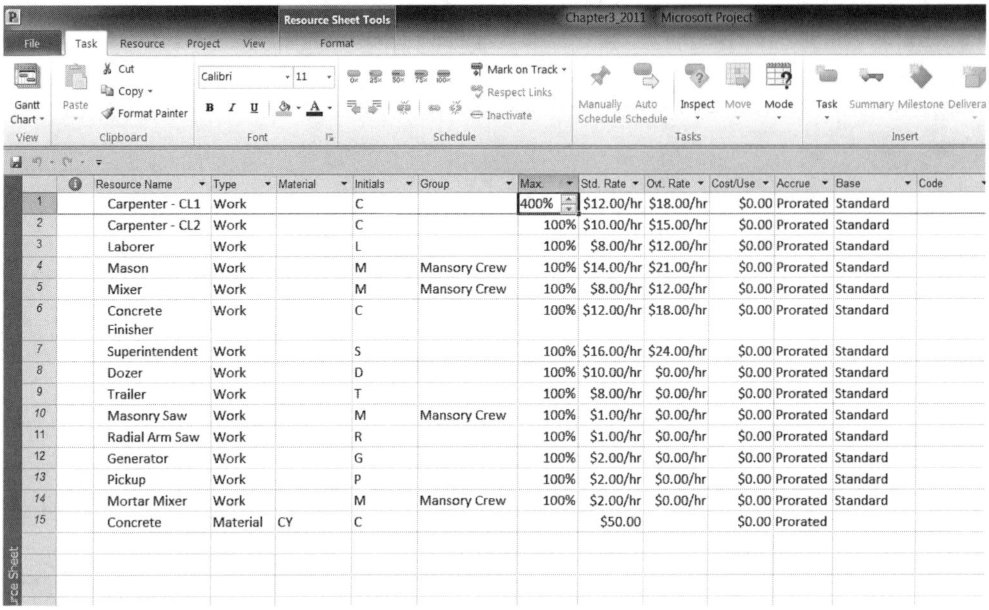

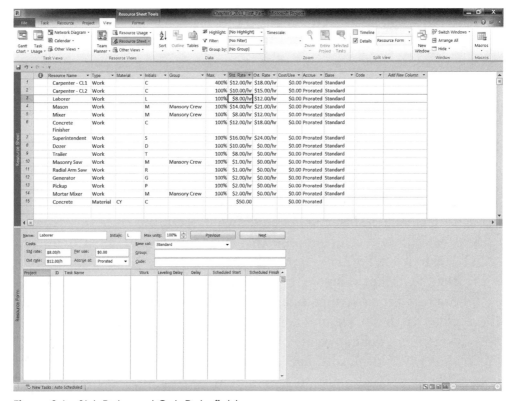

Figure 3.5 Max. Units field

Figure 3.6 Std. Rate and Ovt. Rate fields

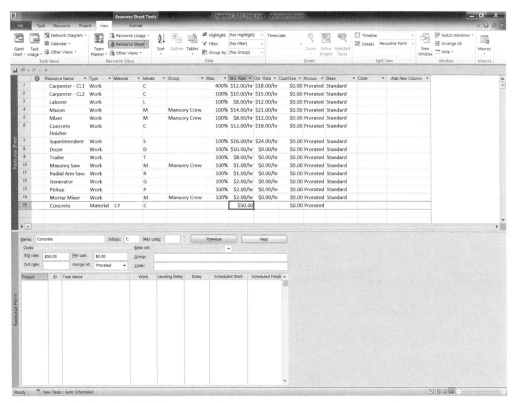

Figure 3.7   Std. Rate field for concrete

The Resource Information dialog box allows you to see all of the pertinent information about a resource (fig. 3.8). To open the dialog box, select the Resource tab on the ribbon and click the Information button or double click the resource in the Resource Name field of the Resource Sheet.

You can use the Resource Availability field in the dialog box to define the availability of resources by calendar restraints. Use the Available From and Available To fields to limit the workdays when a resource can be used. For example, a backhoe might be unavailable on specific days because it is being used on other projects.

By selecting the Costs tab, you can enter different periods to account for future rate changes, such as pay rate changes or material price changes, in the Effective Date field (fig. 3.9). To enter an effective date, click the Effective Date field and select the date from the pop-up calendar. Input the Standard Rate for the new effective date.

Use the Cost Accrual field in the Resource Information dialog box to specify when to account for task and resource costs. To accurately project

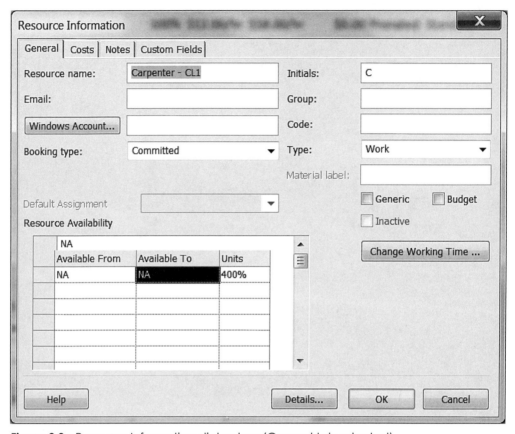

Figure 3.8 Resource Information dialog box (General tab selected)

cash flow, determine whether costs will accrue on individual tasks at their start, end, or while the resource is being used.

Assigning Costs to Resource Lists

Accurate cost information helps you create and control the home building budget. It helps you spot overspending and underspending. Before Microsoft® Project can calculate accurate *resource* costs for a task, you must specify which cost components and calculation methods to use. There are five cost rate tables (labeled A–E) under the Costs tab in the Resource Information dialog box:

- **Rate-based work.** This Work type is one to which you can assign standard cost rates. Microsoft® Project calculates the total resource cost using the following formula:

    rate-based work resource cost = pay rate × time worked

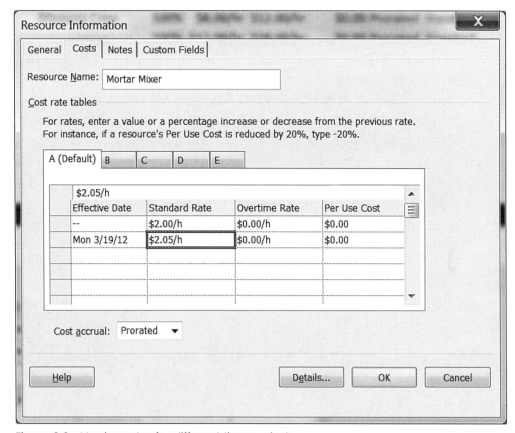

Figure 3.9 Varying rates for different time periods

Assume that a mason costs $14 an hour as shown in figure 3.6. The calculation would look like this:

> $14/hour × 8 hours = $112

- **Rate-based work overtime.** As with rate-based work, rate-based work overtime is a Work type to which you can assign standard cost rates. The mason listed in figure 3.6 costs $21 an hour for overtime. Microsoft® Project will automatically calculate costs associated with overtime pay if you assign hours as overtime work.

- **Rate-based material.** These are Material resources to which you can assign unit cost rates. Microsoft® Project calculates material cost totals as follows:

> rate-based material resource cost = unit cost × quantity of task units

The cost of concrete as shown in figure 3.6 is calculated like this:

> cost of concrete = $50 × 12 CY = $600

- **Per use.** A set, one-time fee for the use of either a Work or a Material resource is a per-use fee. Microsoft® Project assigns the fee each time the resource is used. Both per-use costs and rate-based costs may apply to some resources. For example, the mortar mixer listed in figure 3.8 has a per-use cost of $20. In addition to the $2 hourly standard rate, the user will pay $20 for each use of the mortar mixer. This charge could be for equipment delivery and setup.

- **Fixed.** This is the exact cost of a task. The cost remains constant regardless of the task duration or the work performed by a resource. Whereas a rate-based resource cost will increase when the task takes more time, a fixed cost does not. In figure 3.10, the fixed cost for a trade contractor to paint the exterior of the house is $1,500. You can

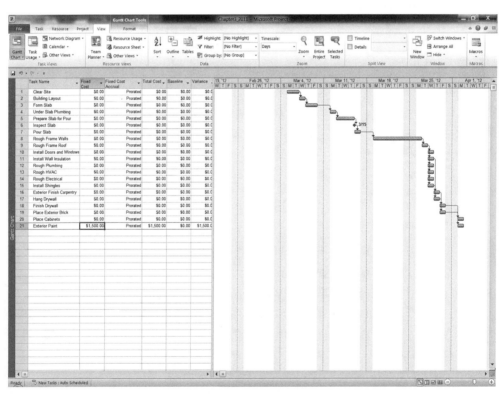

Figure 3.10 Fixed Cost field

use this cost type if you don't want to specify a detailed materials list for a task. Just enter the total cost of each material as a fixed cost.

Skill Practice 3.2 Viewing Costs

- Open Chapter3.mpp.
- Click the View tab on the ribbon.
- Select Gantt chart (fig. 3.11).
- Select Tables. Table: Entry is the default view (fig. 3.12).
- Check Cost (if it has not already been checked) to view the Fixed Cost column.
- Close the file without saving your changes.

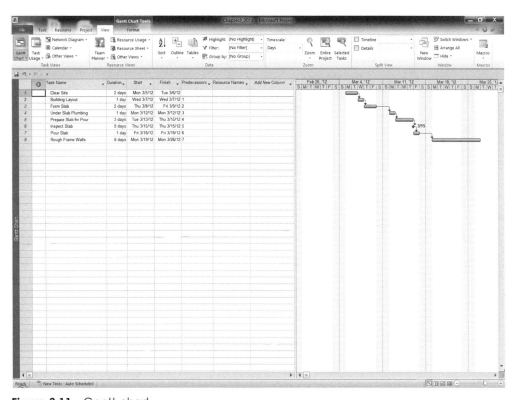

Figure 3.11 Gantt chart

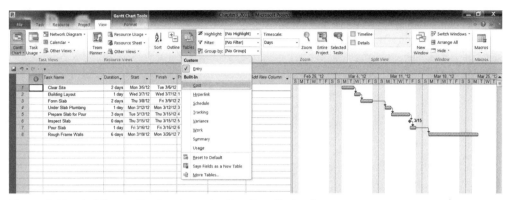

Figure 3.12   Adding a Cost column to the Gantt chart

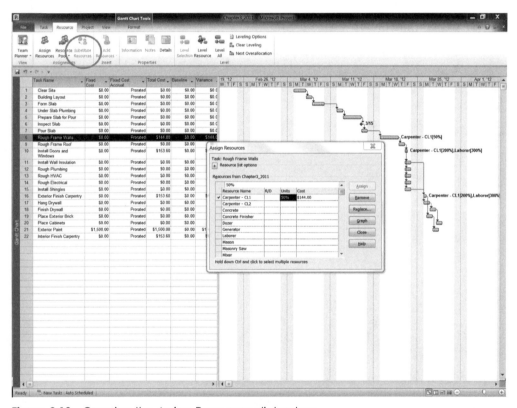

Figure 3.13   Opening the Assign Resources dialog box

Assigning Resources/Costs to Tasks

The Assign Resources dialog box provides the easiest way to create a new resource. You can use this dialog box to enter and assign resources to tasks rather than entering new resources in the Resource Sheet. To access the Assign Resources dialog box, click the Assign Resources button on the ribbon (fig. 3.13).

When using the Assign Resource dialog box to assign resources to a task, select a task and then click the applicable resource. Figure 3.13 shows Rough Frame Walls selected. The default entered in the Units field is 100%, or one unit. The percentages can be changed to decimal equivalents, which allows you to manipulate home building resources simply by increasing or decreasing the maximum units. You may assign partial units to one task and the remainder to another task. For example, with the "Carpenter CL1" units set at 50% as shown, half of the carpenter's time for the day (4 hours) is used on this task. The other four hours could be used elsewhere. If the task required two carpenters, you would input 200% for two full days.

Note that in figure 3.14, 300% is allocated to Carpenter CL1, meaning three full-time carpenters are assigned to this task. Also note that "Carpenter – CL1 [300%]" appears beside the task bar on the Gantt chart. Make sure you don't *overassign* your resources.

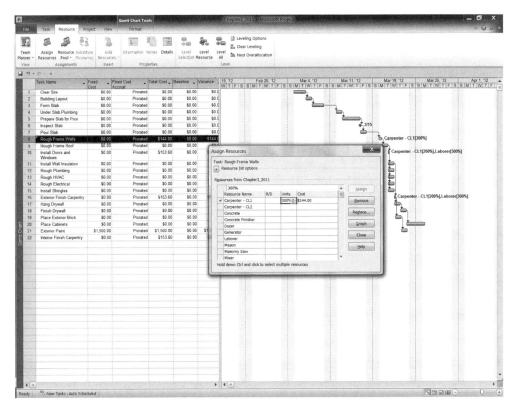

Figure 3.14 Assigning resources

Skill Practice 3.3 Assigning Resources

1. Open Chapter3.mpp.
2. Click the View tab on the ribbon.
3. Click the Gantt chart icon on the ribbon.
4. Select Rough Frame Walls.
5. Click the Resource tab on the ribbon.
6. Click Assign Resources.
7. Assign the Mason resource 150% maximum units.
8. Close the file without saving your changes.

The Task Information dialog box is handy for accessing all task-related information. To open it, click the Task tab on the ribbon and the Information button.

Recurring Resources

You can save time by adding the same resource or resource group to a number of tasks. To do this, press and hold the CTRL key while you click the tasks to which you want to add the resources. The Assign Resources dialog box will appear and you can identify the resource requirements (fig. 3.15). Note that 2 carpenters and 3 laborers were selected. As you assign a resource

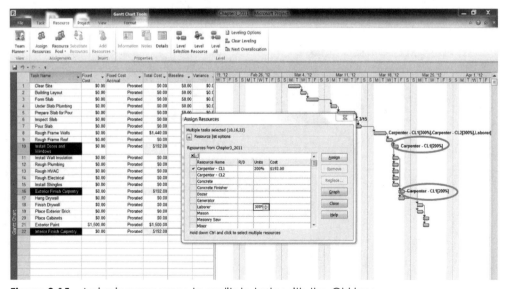

Figure 3.15 Assigning resources to mulitple tasks with the Ctrl key

using the Assign Resources dialog box, the resource appears by the bar for the applicable task on the Gantt chart.

Adding Resource Notes

You will often need to add information to document or clarify project resources. To add resource notes

- Select the applicable resource row.

- Right-click the mouse to access a drop-down menu and click the Notes option (fig. 3.16).

- A dialog box opens (fig. 3.17).

- Enter your note. Microsoft® Project automatically places a note icon in the indicator field (fig. 3.18) of the Resource Sheet when you add a note.

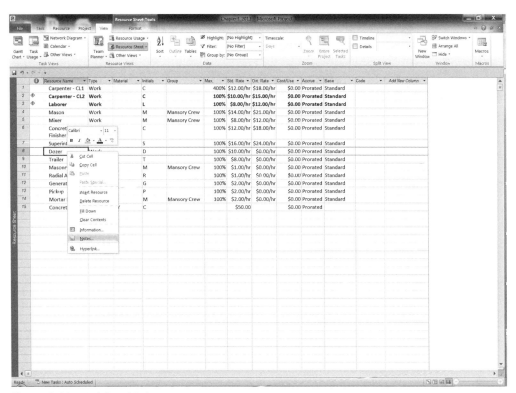

Figure 3.16 Adding Notes

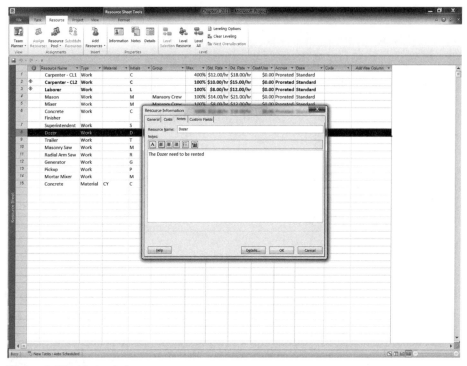

Figure 3.17   Notes tab

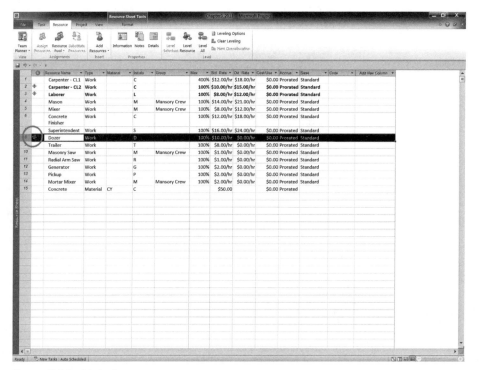

Figure 3.18   Note icon

Managing Resources Efficiently

This chapter showed you how to create a resource list that includes costs and assign resources to the tasks defined in chapter 2. Assigning resources efficiently, including labor, materials, and equipment, is critical to a home builder's success. When you assign resources efficiently, you position yourself to succeed in the competitive market for materials, labor, equipment—and home buyers.

4

Monitoring and Updating the Schedule

You must monitor and regularly update your schedule as a project progresses. This chapter explains how to update and show the progress of a project. You will use the Chapter4.mpp file to practice these skills. This chapter focuses on ways to monitor and update the schedule to ensure the information is current and to document a project's progress. You will learn how to record a home's progress and document changes to a project. Specifically, you will learn how to copy the schedule, establish baselines, access project details, record progress, and change the status date.

Updating the Schedule

Very few projects proceed exactly as planned. Weather, acts of God, productivity rates that are better or worse than anticipated, delivery problems, labor problems, changes in project scope, conflicts between crafts or trade contractors, and work flow mismanagement can alter the best-laid plans. Therefore, you must monitor a project's progress to ensure the schedule is accurate. When you regularly monitor and update your schedule to reflect the actual progress of a project, Microsoft® Project uses this new information to calculate how the changes affect remaining tasks. If a task is delayed, extended, interrupted, or accelerated, Microsoft® Project will show the effects of that change on the task's successors, and all their successors, through project completion. When you update the schedule with the actual progress of a project, Microsoft® Project allows you to compare the current schedule with the original (or baseline) schedule to determine if you are ahead of or lagging behind your target completion date. You must perform the following actions to ensure your schedule is current:

- **Develop a baseline schedule.** The target or original dates are the baseline schedule.

- **Determine a data date.** This date, usually the first day of the new month, is the benchmark for measuring progress. At the beginning of each month, the current schedule should show the history of what was completed and what's left to complete. When you compare the current schedule to the baseline, the update should accurately reflect the current status of the project.

- **Monitor progress.** The focal point of monitoring a project's progress is determining the status of its tasks. Task status can be *complete, partially complete*, or *no work accomplished*. The tasks that have no physical progress keep their original task relationships and durations. Where there is partial physical progress, the schedule maintains the original task relationships and the remaining duration is expressed either as number of days or percentage complete. After you record progress for all applicable tasks as of the data date, the schedule re-calculates. You can then see whether individual tasks and the entire project are on, ahead of, or behind schedule.

- **Update the schedule.** Because projects are seldom built exactly in accord with the original plan, documenting changes is critical to keeping the building schedule current. By tracking changes to the original schedule and devoting time to analyzing these updates, you will understand your current schedule and its implications for project completion. As the construction plan changes, you must modify the schedule accordingly. By changing the schedule to reflect the current plan, you are creating a living document that shows the plan throughout the life of the home construction project. To create a current and effective schedule, you should input revisions regularly as changes occur.

Copying the Schedule

Before you update the schedule, save an electronic copy of the existing schedule on a computer storage device. Besides serving as a backup in the event of a data loss, having this copy allows you to consider "what if" scenarios. If these scenarios turn out to be infeasible, you will still have an original version of the schedule you can recopy and use.

Skill Practice 4.1 Copying a Schedule

1. Open Chapter4.mpp.
2. Click the File menu.
3. Select Save As (fig. 4.1) from the File tab on the ribbon.
4. Rename the schedule "Chapter4 Copy."

You can also use the mouse to copy information from an existing Microsoft® Project schedule into a new schedule as follows.

- Press the right mouse button.

- Select Copy Cell from the drop-down menu that appears.

- Select File, New, Blank Project.

- Press the right mouse button in the cell where you want to copy the information.

- Select Paste from the drop-down menu that appears.

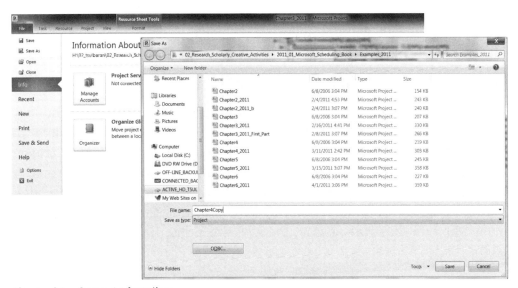

Figure 4.1   Save As function

Setting Baselines

When updating a schedule, Microsoft® Project compares the original schedule (baseline) with the actual schedule to determine physical progress. You can establish new baselines as a project progresses. By setting baselines, you eliminate the need to resave a project file every time task and resource information changes. You can compare a new baseline to a previous baseline (usually the original schedule) in order to understand how changes affect home construction. This helps you identify potential problems, work proactively to solve them, and more precisely estimate task durations and resource requirements as the project proceeds. If you want to compare the baseline to the original schedule, you should create the baseline before you add or update information.

Skill Practice 4.2 Setting a Baseline

1. Open Chapter4.mpp.
2. Click the Project tab on the ribbon
3. Select the Set Baseline drop-down menu.
4. Select Set Baseline. A Set Baseline dialog box appears (fig. 4.2).
5. Select the Set Baseline radio button.
6. Click the down arrow and select Baseline 1. (You can save up to 11 different baselines by clicking on the Baseline drop-down menu.)
7. Click OK.
8. Close the file without saving your changes.

Setting an Interim Plan

After you save the baseline plan and begin updating your schedule you may want to periodically save an *interim plan*. An interim plan is schedule information that saved at a specific point during the project. You can compare the interim plan to the baseline in order to monitor project progress. You can also use an interim plan to document milestones upon which construction draws are based. You might want to save copies of the schedule to document when the slab was poured, the roof was dried in, and the project was completed.

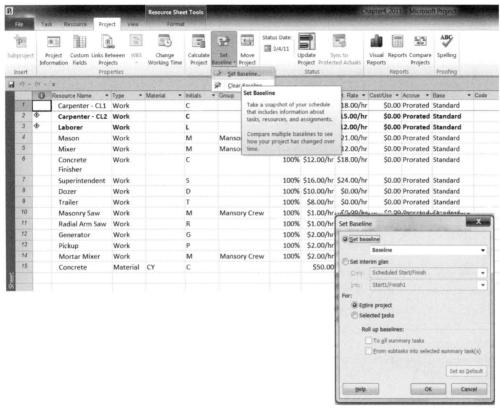

Figure 4.2   Set Baseline dialog box

Skill Practice 4.3 Setting an Interim Plan

1. Open Chapter4.mpp.
2. Click the Project tab on the ribbon.
3. Select Set Baseline drop-down menu (fig. 4.3).
4. Select the Set Baseline option. The Set Baseline dialog box appears.
5. Select the Set interim plan radio button.
6. Select the fields you want to copy to the interim plan from the Copy drop-down menu (fig. 4.4). For example, if you want to create an interim schedule based on current start/finish dates, then use the default options (Start/Finish). If you want to create an interim schedule based on a previous interim schedule, such as Interim 1, then select Start1/Finish1.

7. From the Into drop-down menu, select the fields you want to copy the information to. For example, if you want to create an Interim 2 schedule, select Start2/Finish2.

8. Close the file without saving your changes.

Adding a Task to a Baseline or Interim Plan

You can add tasks during scheduling. If you add a task to the current schedule after you set a baseline or interim plan, you should also add it to the baseline or interim plan so you can track actual versus expected progress. For example, a home builder's original schedule has 50 tasks and this schedule is the baseline used to update the current schedule and assess progress. The builder discovers a new task needs to be added to the current schedule. Because task 51 is not on the original (baseline) schedule, he or she will not be able to compare its actual progress with its scheduled progress unless the task is also added to the baseline schedule. You can add

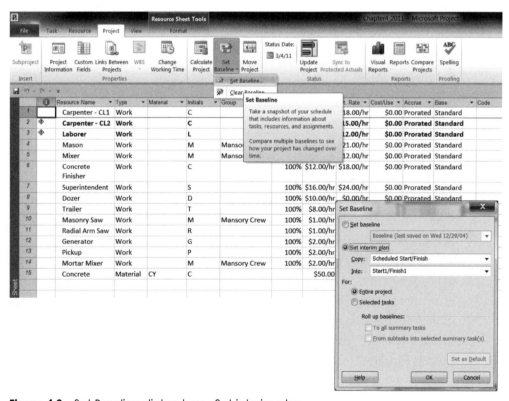

Figure 4.3   Set Baseline dialog box—Set interim plan

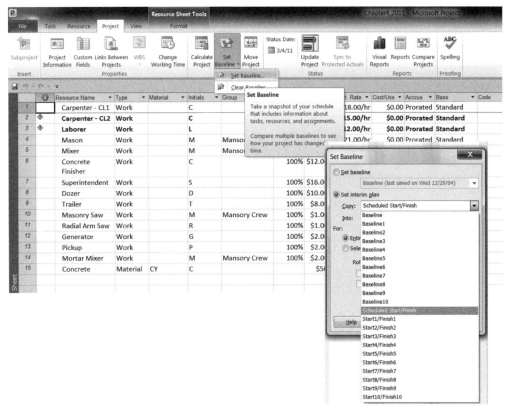

Figure 4.4 Set Baseline dialog box copy menu

a task to the baseline schedule without making any other modifications to the original schedule.

Add a task to the baseline or interim plan as follows:

1. Click the Task Name on the Gantt chart.
2. Follow steps 2–4 in the Baseline practice instructions.
3. Click the Save baseline or Save interim plan check box in the Save Baseline dialog box.
4. Click the Selected tasks check box. If you select Entire project instead of Selected tasks, you will reset the plan for the entire schedule rather than just for the task you added.
5. Click OK.

Follow the same instructions to change the task baseline information. Simply select the Task on the Gantt chart and click the Selected tasks check box in the Save Baseline dialog box. Note that when you click Selected tasks, Microsoft® Project only updates the baseline data for the tasks you selected.

Project Information Dialog Box

The Project Information dialog box allows you to review and edit the information entered at the beginning of the project.

- To use baseline information, click the Project tab on the ribbon
- Select the Project Information button. The Project Information dialog box appears (fig. 4.5).
- Enter a Start date to schedule your project from the start date. The Finish date field is "grayed out." Microsoft® Project will calculate the Finish date based upon the task information that you enter.
- Enter a finish date to schedule your project from the finish date. The Start date field is "grayed out." Microsoft® Project will calculate the Start date based upon the task information that you enter.
- Use Schedule from to develop your schedule from the Project Start Date or the Project Finish Date.
- The Current date is populated.
- Input a Status date to view tasks completed, partially finished, or not started.
- The Calendar options are 24 Hour, Night Shift, or Standard.
- The number in the Priority field indicates the priority that each activity resource will receive when leveled across multiple projects. You can predetermine a whether you want a project to be available for leveling by establishing its priority. For example, if the project you're working on is sharing resources with another project that serves as a *resource pool* and you don't want to level the tasks in one of the files that is sharing resources, then set that *shared file's* priority level to 1,000.
- Clicking the Statistics button (lower left) will display a report showing the impact of updates and changes to the project (fig. 4.6).

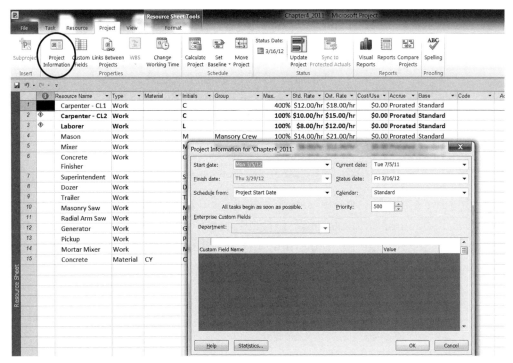

Figure 4.5   Project Information dialog box

Project Statistics for 'Chapter4_2011'

	Start	Finish
Current	Mon 3/5/12	Tue 3/27/12
Baseline	Mon 3/5/12	Tue 3/27/12
Actual	NA	NA
Variance	0d	0d

	Duration	Work	Cost
Current	17d?	192h	$3,400.80
Baseline	17d	192h	$3,400.80
Actual	0d	0h	$0.00
Remaining	17d?	192h	$3,400.80

Percent complete:

Duration: 0%   Work: 0%   Close

Figure 4.6   Project Statistics report

Recording Progress

You can record progress in one of three ways:

1. Enter the actual start and finish dates of the task.
2. Enter the actual duration of a task.
3. Indicate progress as a percentage.

Actual Start and Finish Dates for a Task

Entering the actual start and finish dates for a task creates a history of the work as it occurs. You can use this information to recalculate the home construction schedule for remaining tasks. You can also use this historical information when you create schedules for future home building projects.

Skill Practice 4.4 Entering Start and Finish Dates

1. Open Chapter4.mpp.
2. Select the Clear Site task from the Gantt chart view.
3. Click the Task tab on the ribbon.
4. Select the Mark on Track drop-down menu.
5. Select Update Tasks (fig. 4.7) and the Update Tasks dialog box will appear (fig. 4.8).

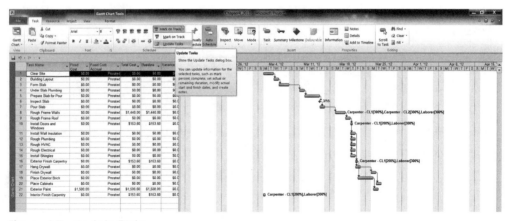

Figure 4.7 Update Tasks

6. Click the down arrow under the Actual Start field to view a pop-up calendar. The baseline plan was to start the task on Monday, March 5, and finish on Tuesday, March 6. Notice that the Clear Site task was actually started on Monday, March 5 and the actual finish date for the task was Tuesday, March 6 (fig. 4.9).

7. Click OK.

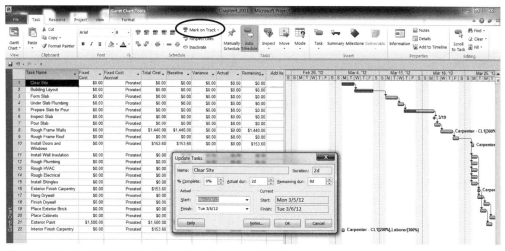

Figure 4.8 Update Tasks dialog box (pre-update)

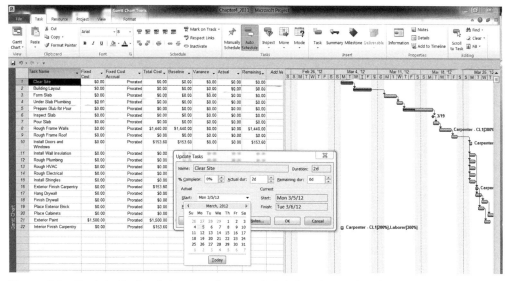

Figure 4.9 Update Tasks dialog box (pre-update) showing calendar

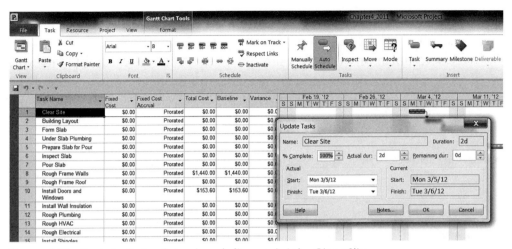

Figure 4.10   Update Tasks dialog box (after update)—Clear Site

Notice the impact of the updated Clear Site task in figure 4.10. Microsoft® Project automatically changed the following fields:

- **% Complete** changed to 100% because the actual finish date was entered, and the task is considered complete.

- **Actual dur** changed from 0d to 2d. The actual duration is from Monday, March 5 to Tuesday, March 6.

- **Remaining dur** changed from 2d to 0d because the actual finish date was entered, and the task is complete.

The entire schedule was updated based on the progress of the Clear Site task. The Clear Site task bar on the Gantt chart has a dark solid line through it that denotes actual progress.

The Task Update dialog box allows you to enter the actual task duration instead of start and finish dates.

Skill Practice 4.5 Entering Task Durations

1. Open Chapter4.mpp.
2. Select the Building Layout task from the Gantt chart view.
3. Click the Task tab on the ribbon.
4. Select the Mark on Track drop-down menu.

5. Select Update Tasks. The Update Tasks dialog box for the Building Layout task appears in the Gantt chart view.

6. Click the Task tab on the ribbon.

7. Select the Mark on Track drop-down menu.

8. Select Update Tasks and the Update Tasks dialog box will appear (fig. 4.11).

9. A task duration of 2d appears in the Actual dur: field. The baseline plan allowed one day (1d) for this task. By entering the updated task duration, you have recorded that the actual progress was one day longer than anticipated (fig. 4.12).

10. Click OK.

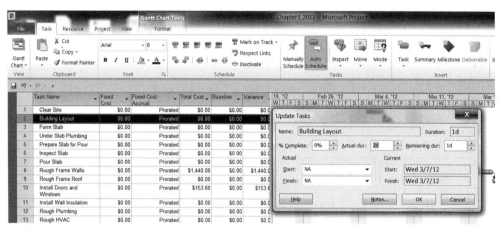

Figure 4.11 Update Tasks dialog box (pre-update)—Building Layout

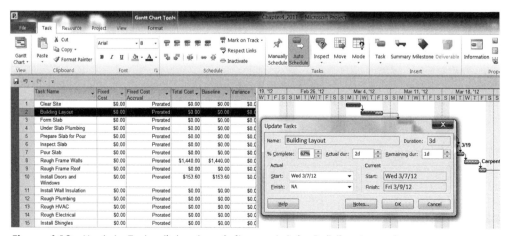

Figure 4.12 Update Tasks dialog box (after update)—Building Layout

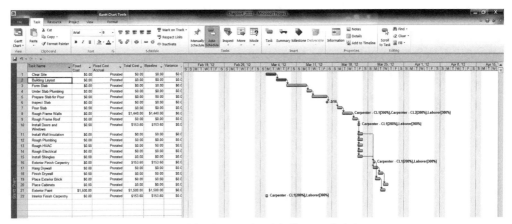

Figure 4.13 Building Layout task in Gantt chart (after update)

Notice the impact of the updated Building Layout task. Microsoft® Project automatically changed the following fields:

- **% Complete** changed to 100% complete because the actual finish date was entered, and the task is complete.

- **Remaining dur.** changed to 0d because the actual finish date was entered, and the task is complete.

Notice that the Building Layout task bar on the Gantt (fig. 4.13) has a dark solid line through it denoting actual progress. All tasks with logic restraints that occur after the Building Layout task now start a day later because of the Building Layout delay.

Indicating Progress as a Percentage

You can also use the Task Update dialog box to enter the progress as a percentage instead of actual task duration or actual start and finish dates.

Skill Practice 4.6 Entering Percentage Completion

1. Open Chapter4.mpp.
2. Select the Prepare Slab for Pour task from the Gantt chart view.
3. Click the Task tab on the ribbon.
4. Select the Mark on Track drop-down menu.

5. Select Update Tasks and the Update Tasks dialog box for the Prepare Slab for Pour task will appear in the Gantt chart view.

6. Click the Task tab on the ribbon.

7. Select the Mark on Track drop-down menu.

8. Select Update Tasks and the Update Tasks dialog box appears (fig. 4.14).

9. Note that the % Complete field contains a value of 66%.

10. Click OK.

Notice the impact of the updated Prepare Slab for Pour task. Microsoft® Project automatically changed the following fields:

- **Actual dur** changed to 1.98d because almost 2 days of the baseline/original 3 days were expended.

- **Remaining dur** changed to 1.02d because a little more than 1 day of the baseline/original 3 days is left to be expended.

- **Actual Start** did not change.

Selecting the Status Date

You can update the schedule using a specific status date. The resulting current schedule will show physical progress as of the date you specify (the current schedule as of the status date) compared with the original (baseline)

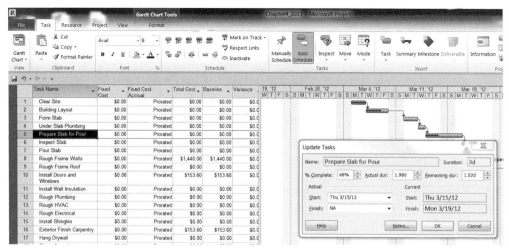

Figure 4.14   Update Tasks dialog box (pre-update)—Prepare Slab for Pour

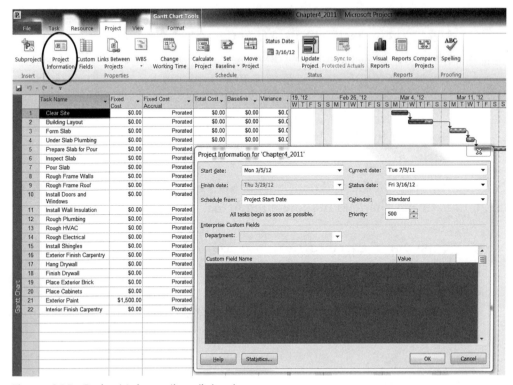

Figure 4.15   Project Information dialog box

schedule. Typically a home builder will use the ending date for a pertinent time period such as a week, a month, or when requirements for progress payments are complete.

Skill Practice 4.7 Setting a Status Date

1. Select the Project tab on the ribbon.
2. Click the Project Information button. The Project Information dialog box will appear (fig. 4.15).
3. Click the down arrow next to the Status date field to set a status date. From the Drop-down calendar select Fri 3/16/12.
4. Click OK.

If you want the Status date line to appear on the Gantt chart, follow these steps:

1. In Gantt chart view, place your cursor on the bar chart.
2. Click the right mouse button. A menu appears.

3. Select Progress Lines (fig. 4.16). The Progress Lines dialog box appears (fig. 4.17).
4. Check the Display box under Current progress line.
5. Click the At project status date radio button.
6. Check Baseline plan in the Display progress lines in relation to options box located in the lower right-hand portion of the Progress Lines dialog box (fig. 4.18). This will allow you to compare the current and baseline schedules. Notice that March 16, 2012, the Status Date, is marked with a vertical line on the Gantt chart (fig. 4.19).

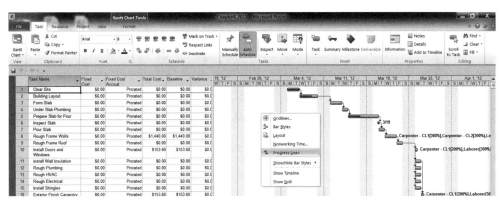

Figure 4.16 Progress Lines

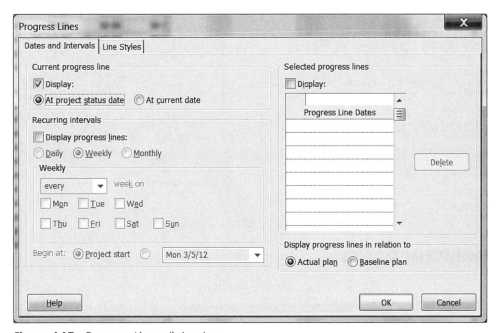

Figure 4.17 Progress Lines dialog box

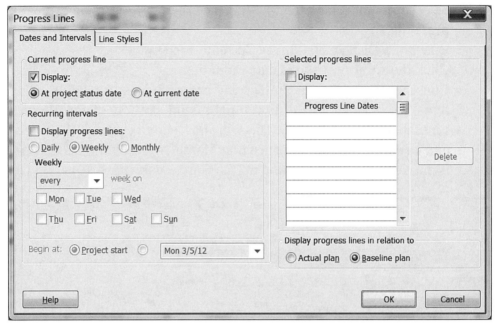

Figure 4.18   Progress Lines dialog box with Baseline plan selected

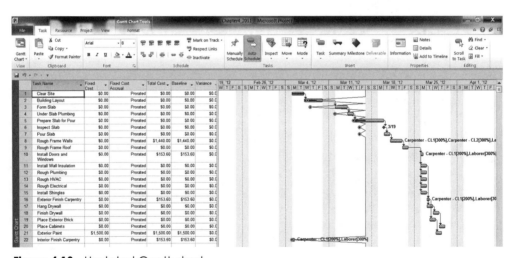

Figure 4.19   Updated Gantt chart

Modifying the Schedule

You must modify the schedule to show changes because it is your baseline home building plan. You can change task durations if your crew size increases. You can also change the logic of task sequences and interrelationships to more accurately reflect interferences. You can add or delete tasks to reflect changes in the project scope, or you may need to add tasks for greater detail. You will find other areas to modify as a project proceeds and you have more information. Whatever their source, you must incorporate changes into the schedule to track and update progress accurately. Generally, using the project name with the current date is the easiest way to organize and access updated schedules.

Knowledge is Power

In this chapter you learned how to use Microsoft® Project to monitor and update your construction schedule. You can establish baselines, make copies of your schedule at significant intervals and milestones, and access detailed project information. By using these features, you can be confident that your schedule is current so you can communicate about it with your trade contractors, home owners, and others with a stake in your project.

5

Updating Task Resources and Costs

Microsoft® Project allows you to update the resources used and cost incurred during construction so you can compare these, for each activity, with the estimate.

After completing this chapter, you will be able to

- compare baseline costs to actual costs;
- use updated cost tables;
- record actual expenditures;
- analyze costs; and
- split tasks.

Use the Chapter5.mpp file to learn how to maintain your schedule by updating work progress and inputting resource and cost expenditures.

Updating Project Resource and Cost Information

If you can track and manage costs to keep your schedule current, your project is more likely to succeed. Project costs comprisc labor, equipment, materials, and other resources. When you develop the baseline schedule, Microsoft® Project assigns these costs to the tasks according to the original estimate. By tracking actual costs and comparing them to the baseline budget, you can determine *cost progress* and *earned value*.

Controlling costs includes determining whether a project is making or losing money according to the baseline plan. Home builders often use cost-loaded schedules and *cost-monitored schedules* to communicate with the home owner. You can use Microsoft® Project to update costs to match up-dated task durations and logic.

To keep your schedule current, you must regularly track tasks and up-date their associated resources and costs. Microsoft® Project facilitates this process. You enter information and the program automatically updates the schedule. After the schedule updates, you can compare the baseline plan with current progress, using bar charts. You can also determine whether tasks are over or under budget by viewing numerical data in various tables.

Comparing Baseline Costs with Actual Costs

The current schedule contains the schedule and logic modifications that you made to update the baseline schedule. It also includes the actual current data and dates, along with your actual resources expenditures. As you acquire actual cost information, enter it into the schedule to reflect the actual cost to date. Comparing the baseline costs to the actual costs of work performed enables you to forecast future costs based on the costs to date and your knowledge of the project.

Using Updated Cost Tables

In Chapter 4, we made task duration and logic changes. Now we must enter the actual cost information for the project. Because Microsoft® Project cre-ates new task cost totals based on duration changes, you must update the schedule with the actual expenditures to forecast future spending.

The Cost Table provides a convenient tool for tracking and analyzing costs. Access it as follows:

- Click the View tab on the ribbon.
- Click Tables. A drop-down menu appears.
- Click Cost (fig. 5.1). A Cost Table appears (fig. 5.2).

Recording Actual Expenditures

As your project progresses, you must record the actual cost expenditures and update your actual costs in Microsoft® Project to compare actual costs with the baseline estimate. This allows you to see whether your project is making

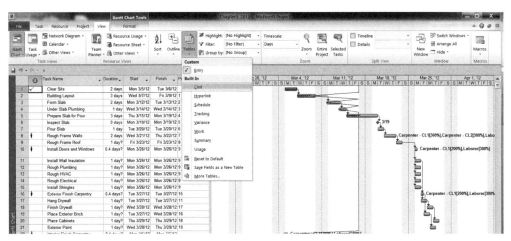

Figure 5.1 Accessing the Cost table

Figure 5.2 Cost table

money (whether expenditures are ahead of or behind schedule). Microsoft®
Project consolidates costs by task. However, most builders gather costs by account rather than by task: timesheets, work measurement reports, purchase
orders, estimates, and all other cost accounting documents use cost account
codes. To collect costs by task, you must add a step to your information
gathering.

Tracking Cost: Actual vs. Baseline Expenditures

You can use the Cost Table to update individual tasks with current actual
cost information. Following is an example, using the Clear Site task.

Table 5.1   Baseline cost for the Clear Site task

Resource	Hours	Cost
Carpenter	(8 hr/day) × 2 days = 16 hrs	16 × $12/hr = $192
Laborer (2)	(8 hr/day) × 2 days × 2 = 32 hrs	32 × $8/hr = $256
Pickup	(8 hr/day) × 2 days = 16 hrs	16 × $2/hr = $32
Dozer	(8 hr/day) × 2 days = 16 hrs	16 × $10/hr = $160
Baseline cost		$640

Clear Site Task

The Clear Site task in figure 5.2 shows a Baseline cost of $640. Remember the Baseline column represents the original plan for the cost required to complete this task. Table 5.1 shows the resources, hours, and costs that comprise the Clear Site task.

The Task Usage view in Microsoft® Project shows the resources for and costs of a specific task.

Skill Practice 5.1 Entering Actual Resource Usage

- Open the Chapter5.mpp file.

- Click the Task Usage button on the ribbon. The Task Usage view shows 80 hours budgeted for the 4 resources (fig. 5.3). You can change the number to reflect actual resource usage.

- Scroll horizontally until you see the March 4, 2012 column.

- Click inside the Dozer Work field and change the value to15 h. Notice how the actual cost information for the Clear Site task and the Laborer resource automatically changed to reflect the time difference.

- Notice how your change affects the schedule:

  ○ **Total Cost.** The actual start and finish dates change to reflect actual progress for the Clear Site task. Because the actual duration of the task is still 2 days, Microsoft® Project did not change the value for this task in the Total Cost column.

  ○ **Actual.** The original costs in the Actual cost column show a cost overrun (fig. 5.4). Here's how the change in the Actual cost to $720 affects the schedule:

    ▪ The Baseline remains the same.

    ▪ The Total Cost increases to $720.

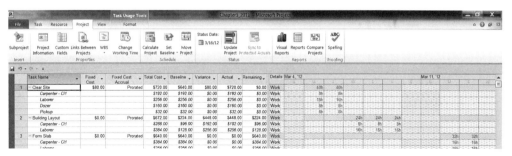

Figure 5.3 Task Usage view

	Task Name	Fixed Cost	Fixed Cost Accrual	Total Cost	Baseline	Variance	Actual	Remaining
1	⊟ Clear Site	$80.00	Prorated	$720.00	$640.00	$80.00	$720.00	$0.00

Figure 5.4 Actual Cost field

- The Variance column reflects the difference between the Total Cost and the Baseline
- $720 (Total Cost) – $640 (Baseline) = $80 (Variance)
- The Fixed Cost increased by $80. Because the resource durations and costs remained the same, Microsoft® Project automatically placed the cost variance in the Fixed Cost column.
- The Remaining column did not change because the activity is 100% complete.

• Close the file without saving your changes.

The Tracking Gantt

The Tracking Gantt provides another useful way to view cost information. From the View tab on the ribbon, click on the Gantt chart drop-down menu and select Tracking Gantt (fig. 5.5).

Figure 5.5 Accessing the Tracking Gantt view

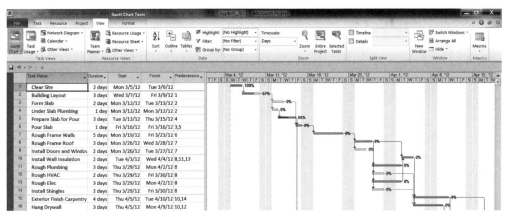

Figure 5.6 Tracking Gantt view

The Tracking Gantt view appears (fig. 5.6). In addition, the Tracking Gantt in the chart on the right shows the actual progress in a solid bar (Clear Site, 100% complete) compared with the baseline schedule in a translucent bar (Form Slab, 0% complete).

Building Layout Task

The Building Layout task has a Baseline cost of $224 (table 5.2).

- **Total Cost.** Note the Total Cost column for Building Layout shows $672 (fig. 5.7). When you updated this task in Chapter 4, you changed the Baseline duration from one day to three days. As a result, Microsoft® Project automatically tripled the requirements for all resources.

- **Actual.** Only 30 hours of laborer time were expended (fig. 5.8), 2 fewer hours than the projected 32. Therefore, the Laborer resource changed from 32 hours to 30 in the Task Usage view. Notice the impact of this reduction on costs (fig. 5.9).

   ○ The Baseline cost remained the same ($224).

Table 5.2 Baseline cost for the Building Layout task

Resource	Hours	Cost
Carpenter	(8 hr/day) × 1 day = 8 hrs	8 × $12/hr = $96
Laborer (2)	(8 hr/day) × 1 day × 2 = 16 hrs	16 × $8/hr = $128
Baseline cost		$224

○ The Total Cost decreased to $432. This new total is less than the amount shown in figure 5.5a because fewer laborer hours were used.

○ The Variance column reflects the difference between the Total Cost and the Baseline.

▪ $432 (Total Cost) – $224 (Baseline) = $208 (Variance).

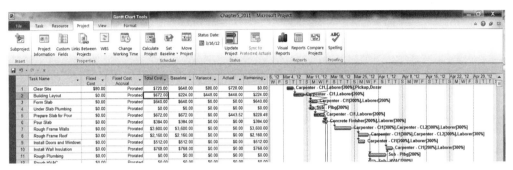

Figure 5.7   Cost Table—Building Layout—Total Cost

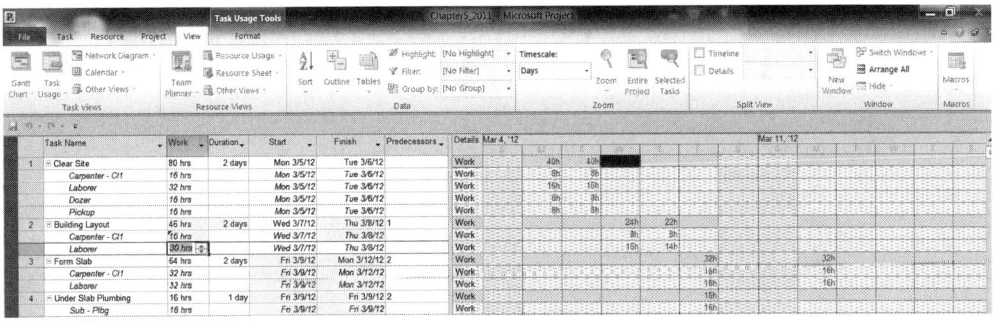

Figure 5.8   Task Usage View—Building Layout—Work Hours

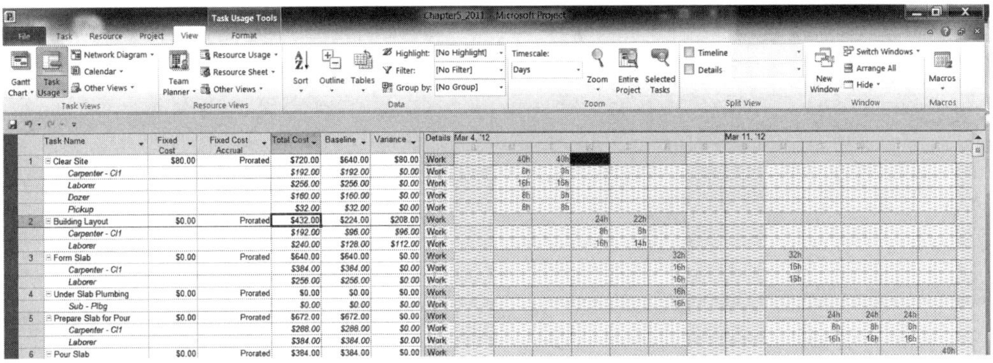

Figure 5.9   Building Layout (after update)

Table 5.3 Baseline cost for the Prepare Slab for Pour task

Resource	Hours	Cost
Carpenter	(8 hr/day) × 3 days = 24 hrs	24 × $12/hr = $288
Laborer (2)	(8 hr/day) × 3 days × 2 = 48 hrs	48 × $8/hr = $384
Baseline cost		$672

Prepare Slab for Pour Task

The Prepare Slab for Pour task has a Baseline cost of $672 (table 5.3).

- **Total Cost.** Note the task Prepare Slab for Pour Total Cost is $672 which is the same as the Baseline cost.

- **Actual.** When the costs were tracked in the field, this task was 66% complete (fig. 5.10).

    - The Baseline column and the Total Cost column remained the same at $672 (fig. 5.11).

    - The Actual cost field reflects $443.52 (66% of $672).

    - The Remaining column shows $228.38 (34% of $672).

Figure 5.10 Prepare Slab for Pour (before update)

Figure 5.11 Cost Table—Prepare Slab for Pour—Total Cost

Figure 5.12   More Tables dialog box

Analyzing Costs

Microsoft® Project allows you to analyze updated costs using the Earned Value table. This tool compares your baseline cash flow with your actual progress. Using it will help you ensure the project doesn't consume more cash than is available to complete it. The Earned Value table displays the actual percentage complete for each task in terms of costs, so you can forecast whether a task will finish over or under budget. When you look at all tasks simultaneously, you can forecast the cost of the house.

View the Earned Value table as follows:

- Select the View tab on the ribbon.
- Click the Tables drop-down menu
- Click More Tables. The More Tables dialog box appears (fig. 5.12).
- Select Earned Value.
- Click Apply.

Figure 5.13 shows the Earned Value table of the Baseline and updated information as entered from the Practice Skill exercises in chapters 3 and 4.

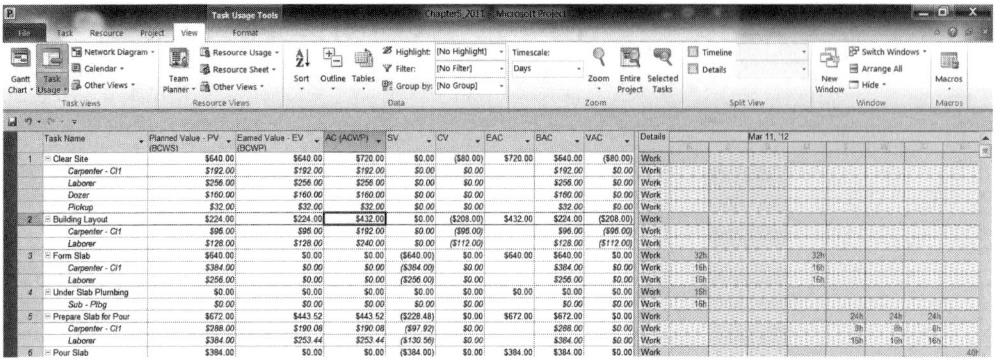

Figure 5.13 Earned Value table

The columns of the Earned Value table, and the data entered in them for the Clear Site task are as follows:

- **Planned Value—PV Budgeted Cost of Work Scheduled (BCWS)** is the baseline (original) budget for the cumulative amount of work to be completed by the status date. The Baseline for the Clear Site task was $640. You can compare the BCWS field to the Budgeted Cost of Work Performed (BCWP) field to determine whether a task's cost is behind or ahead of schedule.

- **Earned Value—EV (BCWP).** This column contains the cumulative value of the *time-phased percent complete* multiplied by the task's *time-phased baseline cost* through the status date. This value is the earned value. The Clear Site is 100% complete. Therefore, according to the baseline plan, 100% of the $640 allotted for the Clear Site task should have been expended.

- **Actual Cost of Work Performed (ACWP)** is the cost incurred for the task through the status date. There was an $80 overrun on the Clear Site task. Therefore, the actual cost of this completed task was $720 ($640 + $80). You determine how and when the ACWP is calculated based on the settings in the Resource Information dialog box, which were discussed in chapter 3.

- **Schedule Variance (SV)** is the earned value of a schedule variance through the status date. The SV is the difference between BCWP and BCWS. The SV is $0 because the baseline and actual duration for the Clear Site task were both 2 days.

- **Cost Variance (CV)** is the earned value of a cost variance through the status date of the schedule. The CV is the difference between the BCWP and the ACWP. Because there was an $80 overrun on the Clear Site task, the CV column shows a value of ($80).

- **EAC (Estimate at Completion)** is the total projected cost for a task. This includes both incurred and future costs. The value in this field is $720 because the Clear Site task is 100% complete. If you had completed 50% of the activity and had incurred a cost greater or less than what was expected ($360), then the estimated cost at completion would have been modified to show the actual expenditure on this task.

- **Budgeted at Completion (BAC)** is the estimated cost of the activity at completion. For example, if you estimate an activity will require 40 hours of work, the wage is $10 per hour, the job requires $300 in materials, and equipment cost is negligible, then the BAC is $700: 40 hrs × $10/hr. (wages) + $300 (materials) + $0 (equipment) = $700

- **Variance at Completion (VAC)** shows the difference between the BAC and the EAC. The value in this field is $80, the total amount of the cost overrun with the Clear Site task 100% complete.

Splitting Tasks

Sometimes you must delay and reschedule home building tasks because resources are temporarily unavailable. Microsoft® Project allows you to pause a task while a resource is unavailable and resume the task when the resource is available. If you need to split a task this way, you should plan to do it in advance. Microsoft® Project will automatically update the partially completed task's actual and scheduled work when you split the task.

To split a task, click the Gantt chart icon on the View tab on the ribbon and click the appropriate task. In figure 5.14, the Building Layout task is selected. Select the Task tab on the ribbon and the broken link button (fig. 5.15). The Split Task dialog box appears (fig. 5.16). Point at the bar of the task you want to split on the Gantt chart. Click and drag the split bar to the right until the appropriate finish split date appears. Select the View tab on the ribbon. Click Gantt chart to see the results of the split task (fig. 5.17). Microsoft® Project will reallocate all resources and costs according to the split.

Figure 5.14 Building Layout task

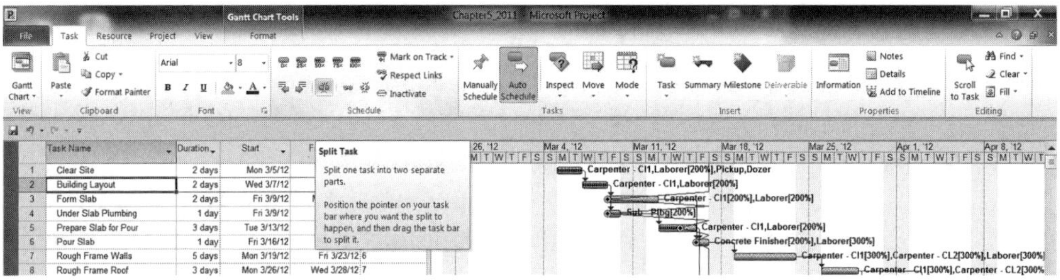

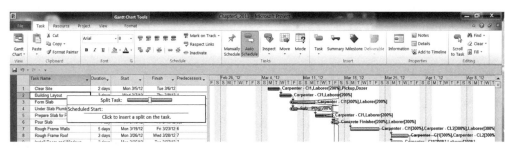

Figure 5.15 Split Task dialog box

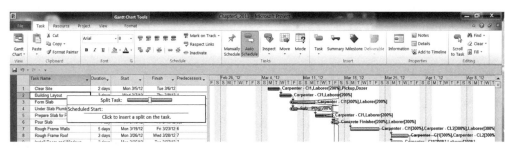

Figure 5.16 Split Task dialog box

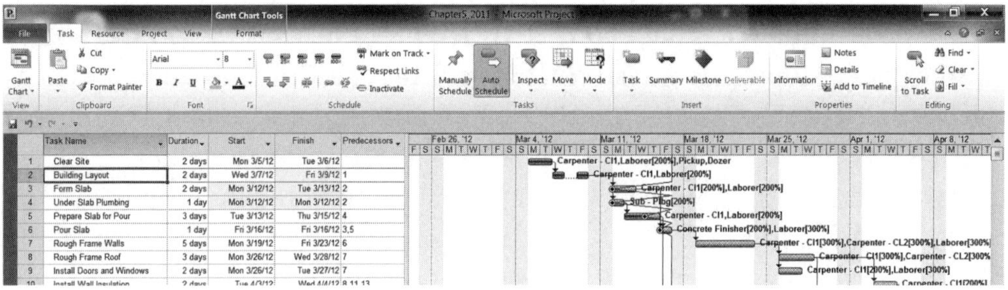

Figure 5.17 Split Task results

Skill Practice 5.2 Splitting a Task

1. Open Chapter5.mpp.
2. Split the Form Slab task.
3. View the results.

Understanding Cost Details

By understanding the costs of your project at any point on the schedule, you can tell whether you are on target, under budget, or over budget so you can make adjustments in real time. The ability to adjust quickly is crucial to making a profit in any economy, whether you are building a custom or inventory home.

6

Generating Reports

This chapter will teach you how to access and evaluate project data and print reports for distribution. Standard reports include calendar view, Gantt chart view and network diagram view. You also can customize some reports to meet the specific needs of your company.

After completing this chapter, you will be able to

- execute prints and copies;
- print views;
- print reports;
- edit reports; and
- copy reports.

Use the Chapter6.mpp file to follow along and perform the practice skills.

Communicating the Schedule

For a schedule to work as planned, you must distribute it and receive feedback about it. Scheduling information—such as timing and sequencing of tasks, their interrelationships, and milestones—is useless if everyone who will participate in the project isn't aware of it. Microsoft® Project allows you to print graphical and tabular views and reports to meet various needs. A graphical report is a pictorial printout of a project's status (such as a Gantt chart) that includes costs, resources, or progress. A tabular report displays information in columns in a spreadsheet.

Figure 6.1   View tab

Executing Prints and Copies

You can print reports using Microsoft® Project default settings or you can create custom reports. Always preview a document on the screen before printing. The preview feature can eliminate paper waste.

- To display Microsoft® Project's print preview, select the View tab on the ribbon and then the view you want to print (fig. 6.1). Select Print from the File menu. The Print Preview will appear at the right of the screen.

- When the file appears as desired, click Print. To leave the Print Preview screen, select any tab on the ribbon.

To produce preconfigured or customized reports, select the Projects tab on the ribbon, and click Reports. Select the report style that best meets your needs. You can use the template reports or create customized reports. You can enhance the visual appeal of your reports by adding headers and footers that include your company logo and the project name. You can also scale information to fit on a single page as shown in figures 6.2 to 6.5. You can print a range of pages (defined by page numbers or dates), suppress blank pages to prevent them from printing, and print multiple copies. If you are running other Microsoft® programs on your computer, Microsoft® Project will use the same default printer the other programs use, or you can select another printer (fig. 6.5).

Viewing Print Area

When printing a view, the number of columns displayed on the screen is the number of columns that will print. For example, if you display the first five columns in the Gantt chart view (ID, Indicators, Task Name, Duration, and

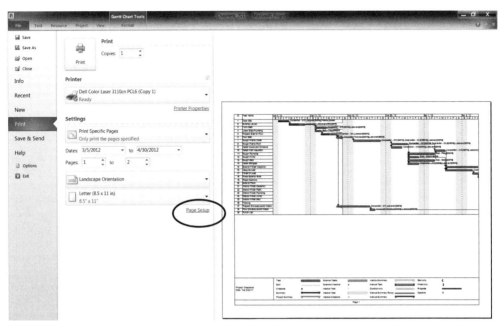

Figure 6.2 Page setup

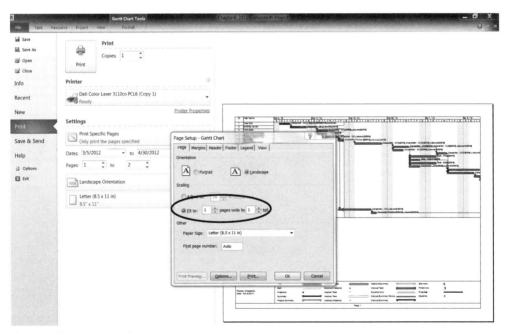

Figure 6.3 Page scaling

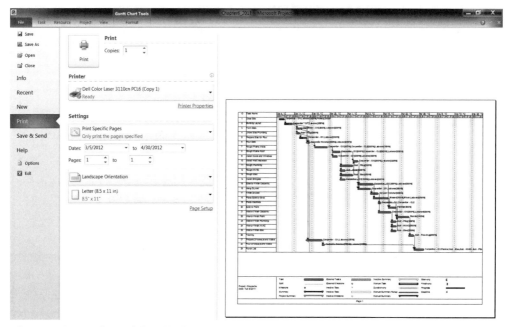

Figure 6.4   Preview of Gantt chart

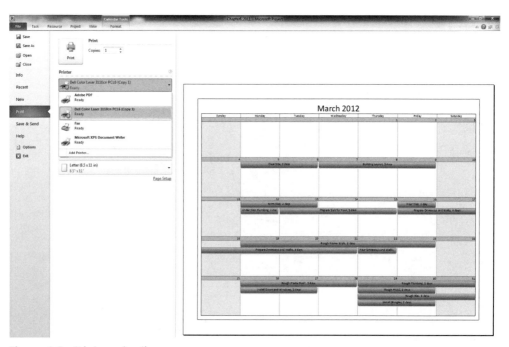

Figure 6.5   Printer selection

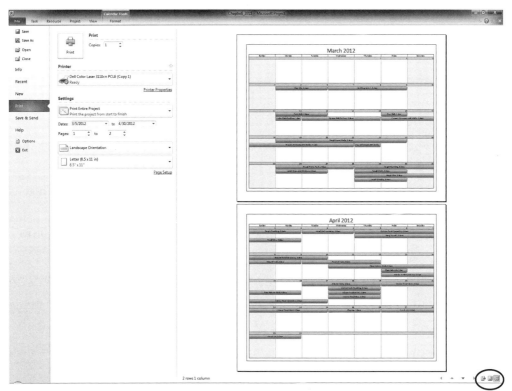

Figure 6.6 Calendar view—zoom

Start), those five columns will appear on the printed pages. In most views, you can specify the number of columns you want to print. Views that are too large to print on a single page are printed vertically and then horizontally, and left to right, starting in the upper-left corner of the view. The pages will be numbered accordingly. Microsoft® Project allows you to move within a view to display additional project information and adjust the timescale in a chart view to display additional graphical information. You can use the Zoom In and Zoom Out buttons located in the lower right portion of the screen (fig. 6.6).

Using different views is the easiest way to change the formatting and display on-screen information. What you see on the screen before going to Print Preview is the view that will appear in the Print Preview. Choose the File button on the ribbon. Select the Print option and the Print Preview of the hard copy report that you will receive appears on the screen.

The on-screen view options are as follows:

- **Calendar.** Allows you to view the project in a monthly calendar.
- **Gantt chart.** Provides an easy-to-use graphical representation of the schedule. Most of the figures in this book are in this view, which home builders commonly use (fig. 6.7).
- **Network Diagram.** Provides a clear picture of the logic flow for task relationships (fig. 6.8).
- **Task Usage.** Allows you to evaluate daily task resource requirements (fig. 6.9).
- **Tracking Gantt.** Provides task progress information along with a graph to show it (fig. 6.10).
- **Resource Graph.** Graphically shows the resource requirements in time units (fig. 6.11).
- **Resource Sheet.** Depicts the resource list for the schedule (fig. 6.12).
- **Resource Usage.** Shows the total usage for each resource by task (fig. 6.13).

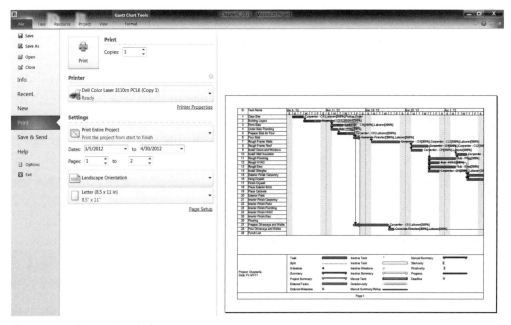

Figure 6.7 Gantt chart view

- **More Views.** When you select this option (fig. 6.14), the More Views dialog box appears (fig. 6.15). You can change views by selecting any of the preconfigured views and then clicking Apply. When you select Print or Print Preview from the File menu, the new view will appear.

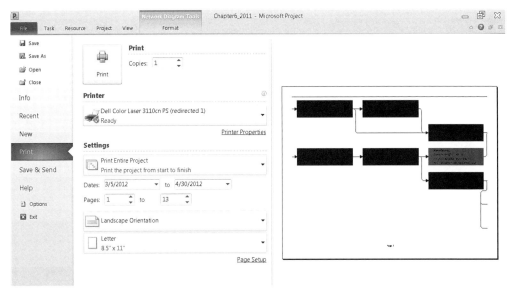

Figure 6.8 Network diagram view

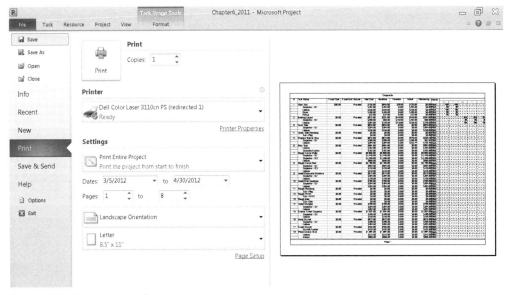

Figure 6.9 Task usage view

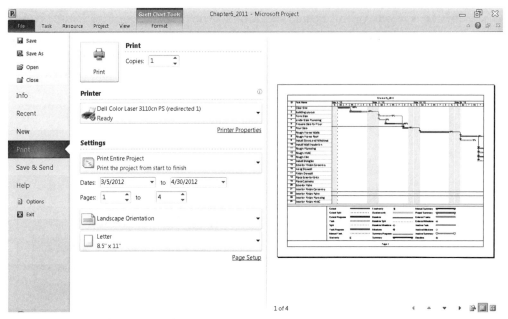

Figure 6.10 Tracking Gantt view

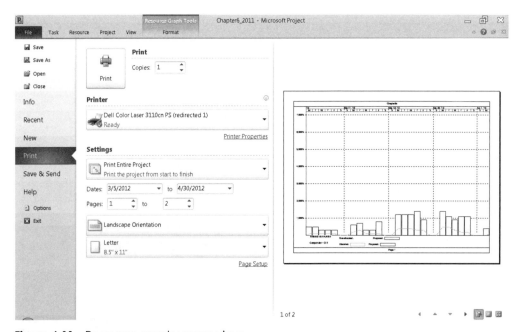

Figure 6.11 Resource graph usage view

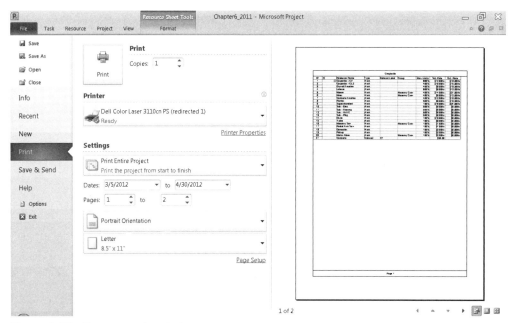

Figure 6.12 Resource sheet view

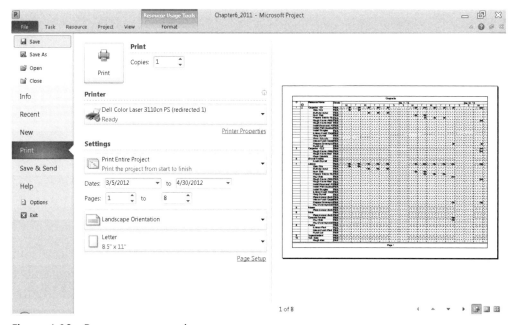

Figure 6.13 Resource usage view

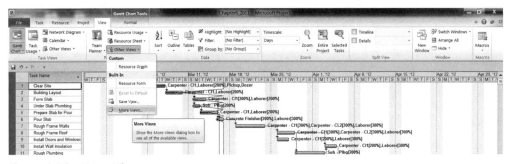

Figure 6.14 More Views

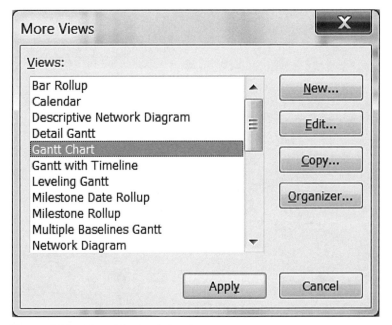

Figure 6.15 More Views dialog box

Projects Tab Reports Button

Microsoft® Project includes 30 preconfigured report types and options you can modify to meet your unique needs. To view all report categories, select the Project tab on the ribbon and click Reports (fig. 6.16). The Reports dialog box will appear with the following six report categories (fig. 6.17).

- Overview
- Current

- Costs
- Assignments
- Workload
- Custom

Overview

Overview reports display information that encompasses the entire project. You can print five different Overview reports:

- Project Summary
- Top-Level Tasks

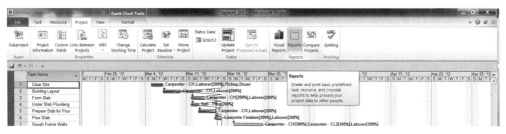

Figure 6.16   Accessing the Reports dialog box

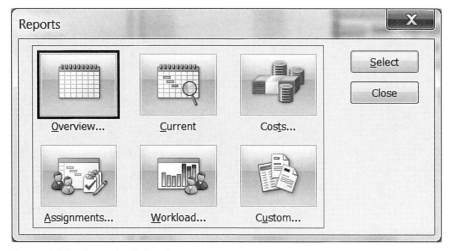

Figure 6.17   Reports dialog box

- Critical Tasks
- Milestones
- Working Days

To access the Overview reports, select the Overview button from the Reports dialog box, and click Select. The Overview Reports dialog box will appear (fig. 6.18). Select the type of report that best suits your needs and click Print. Figure 6.19 is a Critical Tasks report.

Current Activities

Current activity reports show information about the status of certain tasks by category. You can print six different Current Activities reports:

- Unstarted Tasks
- Tasks Starting Soon
- Tasks In Progress
- Completed Tasks
- Should Have Started Tasks
- Slipping Tasks

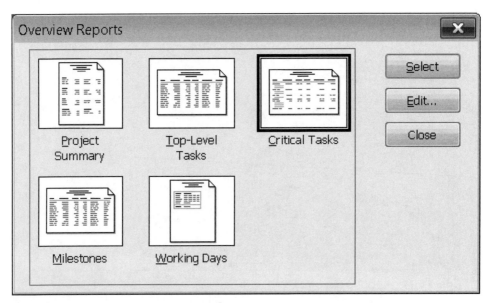

Figure 6.18 Overview Reports dialog box

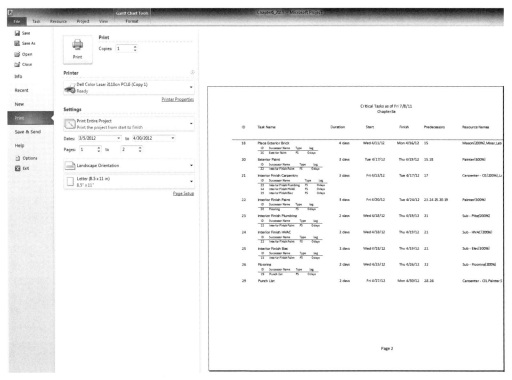

Figure 6.19 Critical Tasks report

To access the Current Activities reports, choose Current Activities from the Reports dialog box (fig. 6.20) and click Select. The Current Activities dialog box appears (fig. 6.21). Select the type of report that best suits your needs and click Print. Figure 6.22 is a Tasks in Progress report.

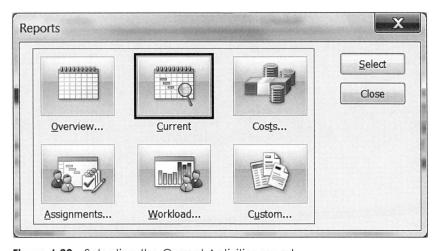

Figure 6.20 Selecting the Current Activities report

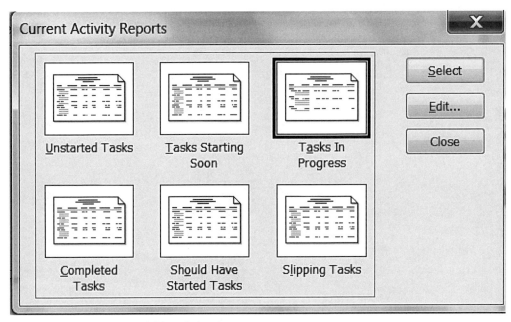

Figure 6.21   Current Activities dialog box

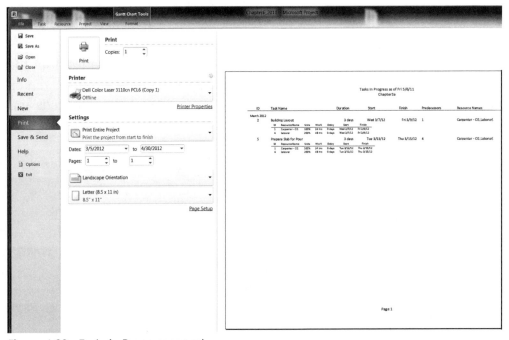

Figure 6.22   Tasks in Progress report

Costs

Cost reports offer financial information about your project. You can print five different cost reports:

- Cash Flow
- Budget
- Overbudget Tasks
- Overbudget Resources
- Earned Value

To access the cost reports, select Costs from the Reports dialog box (fig. 6.23) and click Select.

The Cost Reports dialog box appears (fig. 6.24). Select the type of report that best suits your needs and click Print. Figure 6.25 is a sample Cash Flow report.

Figure 6.23 Selecting Costs reports

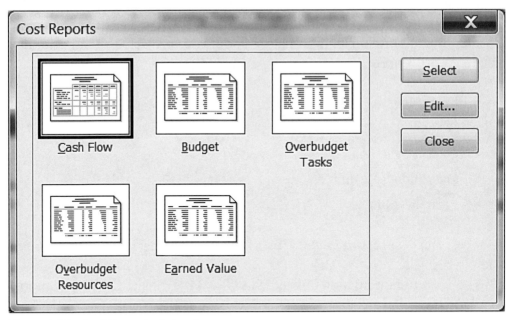

Figure 6.24   Cost Reports dialog box

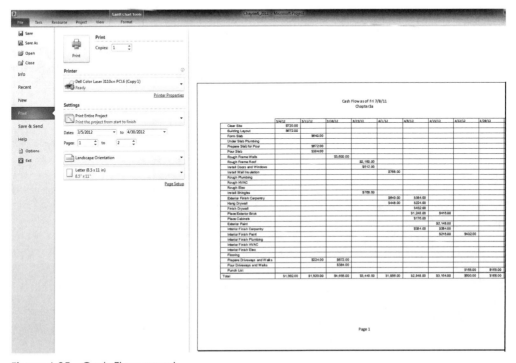

Figure 6.25   Cash Flow report

Assignments

Assignment reports display task resource information. You can print four different Assignment reports:

- Who Does What
- Who Does What When
- To-do List
- Overallocated Resources

To access the Assignment reports, select Assignments from the Reports dialog box (fig. 6.26) and click Select. The Assignment Reports dialog box will appear (fig. 6.27). Select the report you want and click Print. Figure 6.28 is a sample Who Does What report.

Workload

Workload Reports display usage information. You can print two different Workload reports:

- Task Usage
- Resource Usage

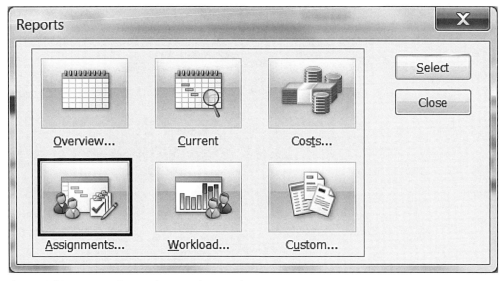

Figure 6.26   Accessing assignments reports

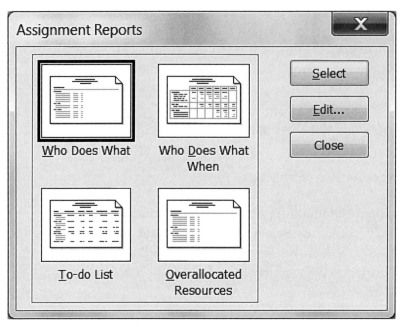

Figure 6.27 Assignments Reports dialog box

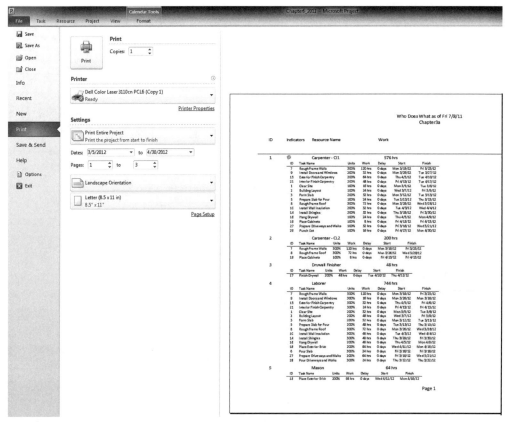

Figure 6.28 Who Does What report

To access the Workload reports, select Workload from the Reports dialog box (fig. 6.29) and click Select. The Workload Reports dialog box will appear (fig. 6.30). Select the type of report that best suits your needs and click Print. Figure 6.31 is a sample Resource Usage report.

Custom

If none of the standard reports meets your needs, you can choose any of eight Custom reports:

1. Base Calendar
2. Crosstab

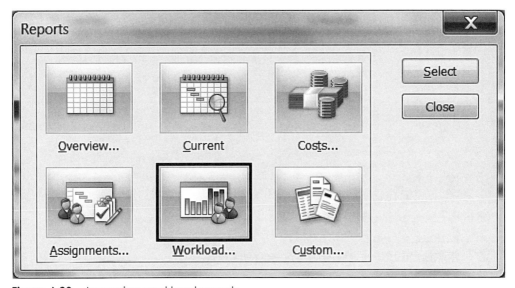

Figure 6.29 Accessing workload reports

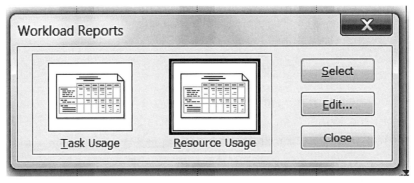

Figure 6.30 Workload reports dialog box

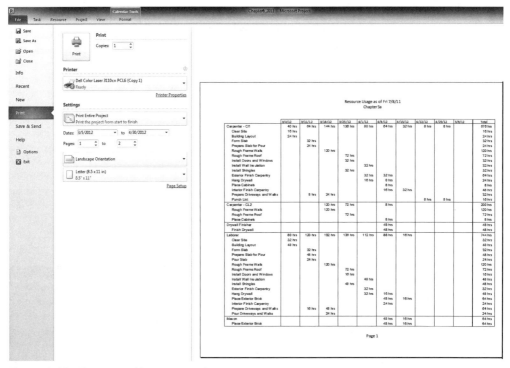

Figure 6.31 Resource Usage report

3. Resource
4. Resource (Material)
5. Resource (Work)
6. Resource Usage (Material)
7. Resource Usage (Work)
8. Task

To access Custom reports, select Custom from the Reports dialog box (fig. 6.32) and click Select. The Custom Reports dialog box will appear. Select the type of report that best suits your needs and click Print.

Skill Practice 6.1 Running Reports

1. Open the Chapter6.mpp file.
2. From the Projects tab, click the Reports button. Select the Overview button and the Critical Tasks option.

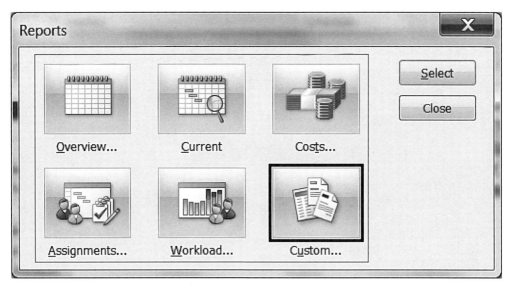

Figure 6.32 Accessing custom reports

   3. Run the following reports:
- Critical Tasks
- Tasks in Progress
- Cash Flow
- Who Does What
- Resource Usage

   4. Print the reports.

Editing Custom Reports

The ability to edit reports to meet your unique needs is a valuable feature. To edit a report, use the Edit button on the right hand side of any reports dialog box.

For example, if you select the Task report from Custom Reports dialog box (fig. 6.33) and click Edit, the Task Report dialog box for the Tasks will appear (fig. 6.34). Most of Microsoft® Project's editing dialog boxes have three tabs:

- Definition
- Details
- Sort

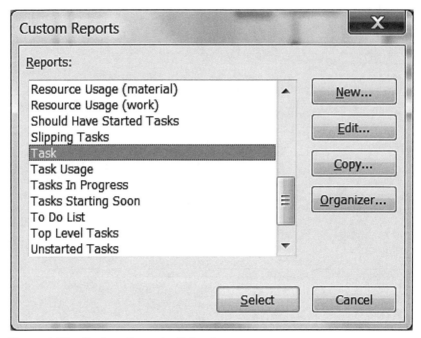

Figure 6.33   Custom Reports dialog box

Figure 6.34   Task Report Definition tab

Definition

The Definition tab is the default. You will use the fields in this tab to select and/or filter the information you want to include in your report. The Period field allows you to specify time intervals for your report. The options are as follows:

- Entire Project
- Years
- Half years
- Quarters
- Months
- Thirds of months
- Weeks
- Days

The Table field allows you to specify which table fields you want to display in your report. The Entry table is the default. The other Table field options are as follows:

- Baseline
- Constraint Dates
- Cost
- Delay
- Earned Value
- Earned Value Cost Indicators
- Earned Value Schedule Indicators
- Entry
- Export
- Hyperlink
- Rollup Table
- Schedule
- Summary

- Tracking
- Usage
- Variance
- Work

The Filter field allows you to narrow the list of tasks and select a group of tasks to display. You can filter tasks as follows:

- All Tasks
- Completed Tasks
- Confirmed
- Cost Greater Than ...
- Cost Overbudget
- Created After
- Critical
- Date Range ...
- In Progress Tasks
- Incomplete Tasks
- Late/Overbudget Task Assigned To ...
- Linked Fields
- Milestones
- Resource Group
- Should Start By ...
- Should Start/Finish By
- Slipped/Late Progress
- Slipping Tasks
- Summary Tasks
- Task Range ...
- Tasks With A Task Calendar Assigned
- Tasks With Attachments

- Tasks With Deadlines
- Tasks With Estimated Durations
- Tasks With Fixed Dates
- Task/Assignments With Overtime
- Top Level Tasks
- Unstarted Tasks
- Using Resource in Date Range
- Using Resource ...
- Work Overbudget

If you click the Text button (fig. 6.35), the Text Styles dialog box will open (fig. 6.36). Use it to specify the font characteristics for your report.

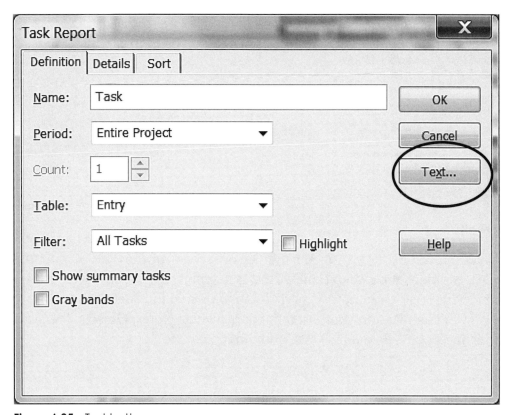

Figure 6.35 Text button

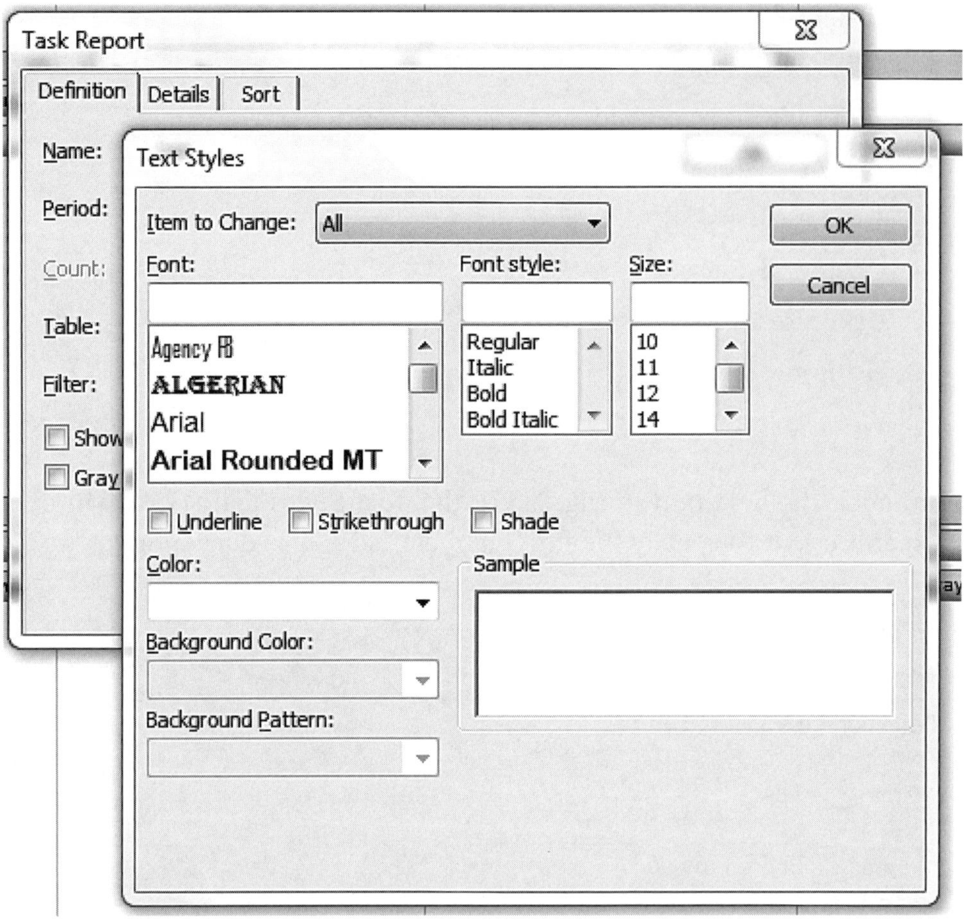

Figure 6.36   Text Styles dialog box

Details

Select the Details tab to obtain the Details screen of the Task Report (fig. 6.37). Although the example shows the Task report, the Details tab works the same with other Custom reports. This tab allows you to specify the elements you want to appear on your printed report such as Notes, Objects, Predecessors, Successors, Schedule, Cost, and Work.

Sort

Select the Sort tab to obtain the Sort screen of the Task report (fig. 6.38). Although this example shows the Task report, the Sort tab works the same

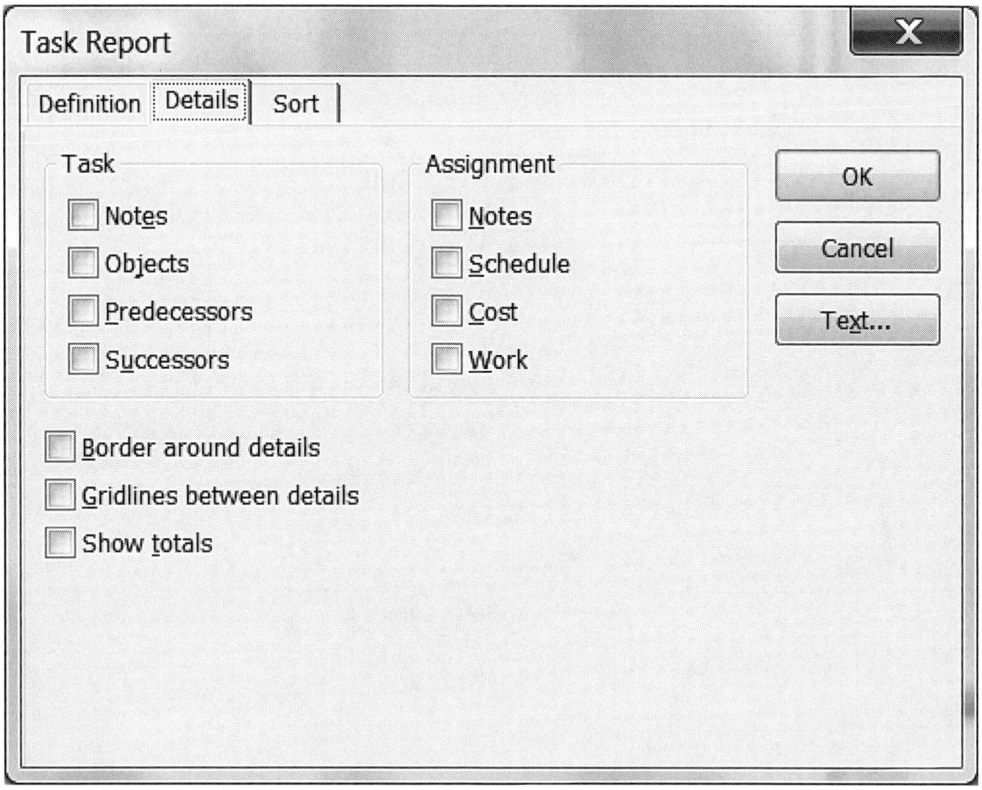

Figure 6.37 Task Report Details tab

with other Custom reports. The Sort tab allows you to change the task sort criteria. There are three levels of sort specifications. After you've selected priority sort criteria in the Sort by field, you can filter the information further by entering information in one or both of the Then by fields.

The Sort by field options are as follows:

- %—Complete, Work Complete
- Actual—Cost, Duration, Finish, Overtime Cost, Overtime Work, Start, Work
- ACWP
- Assignment—Delay, Units
- Baseline—1 to 10—Costs, Duration, Finish, Start, Work
- BCWP
- BCWS

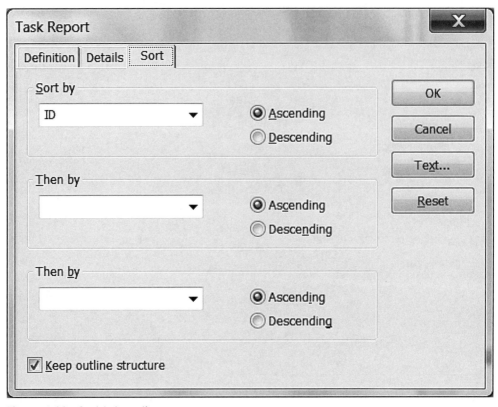

Figure 6.38 Sort tab option

- Constraint—Date, Type
- Contact
- Cost—1 to 10, Rate Table, Variance
- CPI
- Created
- Critical
- CV, CV%
- Date—1 to 10
- Deadline
- Duration—1 to 10, Variance
- EAC
- Early Finish

- Early Start
- Earned Value Method
- Effort Driven
- Estimated
- External Task
- Finish—1 to 10, Slack, Variance
- Fixed Cost—Accrual
- Flag—1 to 20
- Free Slack
- Hide Bar
- Hyperlink—Address, Href, SubAddress
- ID
- Ignore Resource Calendar
- Late—Finish, Start
- Level Assignments
- Leveling—Can Split, Delay
- Linked Fields
- Marked
- Milestone
- Name
- Notes
- Number—1 to 20
- Objects
- Outline Code—1 to 20, Level, Number
- Overallocated
- Overtime—Cost, Work
- Physical % complete
- Predecessors
- Preleveled—Finish, Start
- Priority

- Project
- Recurring
- Regular Work
- Remaining—Cost, Duration, Overtime Cost, Overtime Work, Work
- Resource—Group, Initials, Names, Phonetics, Type
- Resume
- Rollup
- SPI
- Start—1 to 10, Slack, Variance
- Status
- Stop
- Subproject—File, Read Only
- Successors
- Summary
- SV
- Task Calendar
- TCPI
- Text—1 to 30
- Total Slack
- Type
- Unique—ID, ID Predecessor, ID Successor
- VAC
- WBS
- Work—Contour, Variance

The most common sort fields are Early Start and Critical because most home builders want to know the earliest they can start a task and which task(s), if delayed, could extend the overall duration of the project.

Copying Reports

The Copy button is only available from the Custom Reports dialog box. After you print a report, you can make copies of it later. If you don't specify a new name for the copied report, Microsoft® Project will automatically insert "Copy of" in front of the existing file name. For example, if you make a copy of the Task report and don't rename the file, the file name "Copy of Task" will appear in the Custom Reports list.

Skill Practice 6.2 Copying Reports

1. Open Chapter6.mpp.
2. From the Projects tab, select the Reports button. Select the Custom button, select the Task report, and select the Copy button.
3. Click Custom.
4. Click Select.
5. In the Reports list, choose the report you want to copy, and click Copy.
6. Type "Practice Report" in the Name box.
7. Click OK.
8. Your new report should appear in the Custom Reports list.

Using Reports to Communicate

This chapter explained how to print standard and customized reports about a home building project. These reports are essential to enable you to continuously communicate with vendors, trade contractors, customers, lenders, and others about your project. Knowing how to format, print, and distribute reports about your project allows you to demonstrate that you are a professional builder with detailed knowledge about each home you build.

Glossary

baseline. A point of reference with which progress can be measured or compared

baseline schedule. The schedule generally created at the beginning of a project that is a benchmark for project progress and contract performance

complete. A task with all elements accomplished (100%)

cost progress. Records that shows the cost of construction work performed

cost-loaded schedule. A schedule that includes the builder's costs, subcontracting costs, indirect costs, and profit.

cost-monitored schedule. The process of inputting actual costs into tasks and comparing them to planned or estimated costs to determine construction performance

critical path. The critical or longest task path (timewise). It corresponds to the sequence of tasks that have no (zero) float. Tasks on the critical path will delay project completion if they are not completed on time.

critical tasks. Tasks with zero float. If these tasks are not completed on time according to the planned finish date, the project will be delayed.

earned value. A method of measuring project performance. It compares the amount of work that was planned with what was actually accomplished to determine whether cost and schedule performance is as planned.

finish-to-finish (ff) dependency. Given two tasks, the second task cannot be finished before the first task is completed.

finish-to-start dependency (FS). Given two tasks, the second task cannot start until the first task is completed.

flexible. Without a date-specific constraint. For example, a task with a deadline to start "as soon as possible."

Gantt chart. A bar chart in which each bar represents a project task. The Gantt chart illustrates the start and finish dates for each task. The length of each bar represents the task's duration.

inflexible. A date-specific constraint. For example, a specific task must start on July 1.

leveling. A process performed in preparing a schedule that balances the use of resources (usually people or equipment) over time to avoid possible over-allocation of resources

link line. A line that connects two tasks.

no work accomplished. A task with no work completed (0%)

milestone. A major event, phase, or any other important point in the project.

overassign. To assign resources that are not available to an activity.

partially complete. A task with less than 100% of its elements accomplished

phase. A major aspect of the life cycle of a project. Possible life cycle phases are feasibility study, conceptual design, detailed design, bidding, and construction. Time and the control of time relates to all phases of the home project life cycle.

predecessor. A task that must start or finish before another specific task can start or finish

relationship line. A link line that explicitly indicates predecessor and successor tasks.

resource. Labor hours, bulk materials, construction equipment, and permanent equipment.

resource limit. The maximum amount of a resource that is available at one time. For example, if four carpenters are available full time, you can assign the carpenter resource, theoretically, at 400%.

resource pool. The array of resources available to complete a project

ribbon. The menu of program functions located across the top of a Microsoft® Project file

schedule. A document on which a project planner identifies all tasks (with their corresponding durations, relationships, and resources) needed to complete a project.

schedule of values. A type of schedule that allocates values for various tasks and is used as the basis for submitting and reviewing progress payments

shared file. A file using resources from another file, which can be another project file or a file containing only resource information, called a resource pool.

successor. A task that must wait for another task to start or finish before it can be started or finished

start-to-start (SS) dependency. Given two tasks, the second task cannot start until the first task starts.

start-to-finish dependency (SF). Given two tasks, the second task cannot finish until the first task starts.

task. An activity that consumes resources and contributes to project completion

task name. Brief description of a task

task cost-loaded schedule. A schedule in which each task cost has been assigned. The total cost of all the tasks correspond to the expected total cost of the project.

timescale. A scale that specifies the size (on the screen or on paper) that will represent a division of time (i.e., hours, days, weeks).

time-phased percent complete. The amount of the task that is physically completed (e.g., concrete in place) measured in time (i.e., hours, days, weeks) with respect to the overall duration of the task.

time-phased baseline cost. The original estimated cost over the planned (baseline) project period

unit. The unit of measure (e.g., square feet, cubic feet, inches) assigned to a resource or the increment by which you assign and use it.

Index

Resources

Construction Management

Rogers, Leon. *Basic Construction Management: The Superintendent's Job.*
   Washington, DC: NAHB BuilderBooks, 2009.

Contracts and Law

Home Builder Contracts & Construction Management Forms, compiled
   by NAHB Business Management and Information Technology
   Committee. Washington, DC: NAHB BuilderBooks, 2006.
Jaffe, David S., David Crump, and Felicia Watson. *Warranties for
   Builders and Remodelers, Second Edition*. Washington, DC: NAHB
   BuilderBooks, 2007.

Estimating

Christofferson, Jay P. *EstimatorPRO™ 5.2*. Washington, DC: BuilderBooks.
   com, 2010.
——. *Estimating with Microsoft® Excel, Third Edition*. Washington, DC:
   NAHB BuilderBooks, 2010.
——. *Estimating with Microsoft® Excel, Second Edition*. Washington, DC:
   NAHB BuilderBooks, 2003.

Financial Management

Cost of Doing Business Study, 2012 Edition, by NAHB Business
   Management & Information Technology Committee. Washington, DC:
   NAHB BuilderBooks, 2012.
Shinn, Emma. *Accounting and Financial Management for Residential
   Construction*, 5th Edition. Washington, DC: NAHB BuilderBooks,
   2008.

Land Development

*Green Models for Site Development: Applying the National Green
   Building Standard™ to Land and Lots*, by NAHB Land Development.
   Washington, DC: NAHB BuilderBooks, 2011.

Kone, Daisy Linda. *Land Development, 10th Edition*. Washington, DC: NAHB BuilderBooks, 2006.

Marketing and Sales

Flammer, Carol M. *Social Media for Home Builders 2.0: It's Easier Than You Think*. Washington, DC: NAHB BuilderBooks, 2011.

Gullo, Gina and Angela Rinaldi. *Option Selling for Profit: The Builder's Guide to Generating Design Center Revenue & Profit*. Washington, DC: NAHB BuilderBooks, 2008.

Lynch, Tammy. *Think Sold! Creating Home Sales in Any Market*. Washington, DC: NAHB BuilderBooks, 2009.

Nowell, William J., *ValueMatch™ Selling for Home Builders: How to Sell What Matters Most*. Washington, DC: NAHB BuilderBooks, 2009.

Smith, Carol. *Beyond Warranty: Building Your Referral Business*. Washington, DC: NAHB BuilderBooks, 2008.

Webb, Bill. *Sweet Success in New Home Sales: Selling Strong in Changing Markets*. Washington, DC: NAHB BuilderBooks, 2006.

Scheduling

Marchman, David and Tulio Sulbaran. *Scheduling for Home Builders with Microsoft Project*. Washington, DC: NAHB BuilderBooks, 2006.

Warranty

Residential Construction Performance Guidelines, 4th Edition, Contractor Reference by National Association of Home Builders. Washington, DC: BuilderBooks.com, 2011.

Residential Construction Performance Guidelines, 4th Edition, Consumer Reference by National Association of Home Builders. Washington, DC: NAHB BuilderBooks, 2011.

Smith, Carol. *Homeowner Manual: A Template for Home Builders, Second Edition*. Washington, DC: NAHB BuilderBooks, 2000.

Your New Green Home and How to Take Care of It: Homeowner Education Manual Template, by National Association of Home Builders. Washington, DC: NAHB BuilderBooks, 2011.

Your New Home & How to Take Care of It. Washington, DC: NAHB BuilderBooks, 2006.

All of these books are available at www.BuilderBooks.com.